To:

Enjoy the KEG!
Best Wishes!

BEYOND THE MIC

Rob Daniels

ROB DANIELS

Copyright © 2021 by Robert Shatzky

All rights reserved.

No part of this book may be reproduced in any form or by any electronic or mechanical means, including information storage and retrieval systems, without written permission from the author, except for the use of brief quotations in a book review.

This book does not replace the advice of a medical professional. Consult your physician before making any changes to your diet or regular health plan.

CONTENTS

Preface	v
1. Introduction	1
2. Chronic Pain	3
3. Anti-Semitism in America	7
4. Marilena	25
5. Radio	31
6. Mom & Dad	71
7. Intermittent Fasting	77
8. Seasonal Affective Disorder	87
9. Keep Dreaming - Dedicated to the Field Of Dreams Movie Site in Dyersville, Iowa	93
10. My Brother the Blessing	109
11. Anxiety, Obsession & Depression	113
12. Dad Life	125
13. Should I Stay or Should I Go? A Covid-19 Confession	127

PREFACE

"After 20 years of being on Canadian radio Rob Daniels goes beyond the microphone." Throughout the last two decades and still to this day I've tried my best to make being a great radio personality all about the listener on the other end. I want that person to have a good time. They deserve the shining star and are the reason I'm so lucky to be able to do what I do for a living. I fully understand that they are the customer, and I will continue to try and do whatever it takes to keep them happy.

With that being said, have you ever wondered who it really was that's been talking to you on the other end for all these years? Most of my time on the air has been spent over ten second intros of songs, therefore you've received mostly small bursts of my personality, and that's perfectly ok. At the same time, I'm really happy to tell you that this book is an extension of those small bursts, who I am as a whole, what I've been through over the years, and how I try to persevere in this gift we call life.

Hopefully you find it inspiring and useful for your own life. You see, every radio host has a unique and different story. This is mine along with some very valuable tips, advice, and information that just

Preface

might help you out on your own path to success, good health, and happiness.

"A book about falling down seven times, and standing up eight."

Rob Daniels' Beyond The Mic. is also what he calls "Many untold stories revealed and advice to help better your life. He could never fit all that over a song intro or talk break."

I thank you in advance for picking up this book. It would mean the world to receive your feedback. Please enjoy Rob Daniels' Beyond the Mic.

1
INTRODUCTION

There's no limit as to how many stage names one person can have, but after a couple of them it does start to get a little strange. In my case, I feel like I've had good reasons for these. It all started out as Robert Ian Shatzky—my real name—born on the evening of December 2nd, 1983 in downtown Toronto, Ontario, Canada. My parents named me Robert but thought "Robbie" was better suited for an infant and a child, so Robbie stuck all throughout childhood.

At 16 years old I started out on the air at my high school radio station; I went with the alias Rad Tad Rob. That name then turned into Rob Kelly and I couldn't use Rob Kelly on the first professional radio station I was hired at due to there being a co-worker of mine with the same last name already on the air. So, then the birth of Rob Daniels came to light thanks to a radio industry friend of mine. The stage name Rob Daniels has been in place now for the last 17 years or so along with some different variations of the name.

Some people have asked, "Why not just use your real last name on the air?"

I love my real last name, I really do, however I never really thought it meshed well in between music stars on top forty radio.

When I lived in Montreal and worked in radio there, another Rob just so happened to be a host there, so I went with the initials RJ and RJ would also be allowed the moniker RJ Daniels. I moved back to Toronto though, in my mid-twenties, the name Robbie D was suggested to me. It fit the radio station format a little better at the time as they were targeting a younger audience. So Robbie D it was!

    When I ended up at the next radio station that I worked at, I circled back to the name Rob Daniels. I feel like the name Rob Daniels is more universal and fits quite the variety of radio formats and content creation platforms, whereas Robbie D would not. Now, when it comes to the love of my life, my wife Marilena, she calls me Rob. She likes Rob best. It's weird, in all of this I still put Robbie at the top of my list for what I like to be referred to as, but I'm also good with Rob and I'll stick with Robert just for legal documentation and doctors' appointments please and thank you.

2

CHRONIC PAIN

My incredibly wonderful Uncle Allan who has managed a great deal of pain over the years once told me that pain is inevitable, but suffering is optional. As much as I knew he was right, I still hated hearing it. What can I say, I'm stubborn sometimes and when you're in a great deal of pain you almost feel like nobody will understand.

Nevertheless I do carry his words closely with me every day to try and cope, and if you're a chronic pain sufferer, you most likely understand why. Life on Lyrica is how I have referred to it over the years for some of my physical pain that I manage daily. Even though I don't know if I'll be on the medication forever, it just kind of seems that way.

Lyrica is a medication that treats neuropathic pain. It offers you the chance at daily pain management by masking your symptoms-if the medication is effective for you. There is no guarantee. Over the last few years I've battled my mind in regards to taking Lyrica. On the one hand, there are certain days it has worked wonders and on the other hand there are days it didn't work so well. *And* what happens is the medication actually spikes your appetite, so there's a good chance you'll gain some weight unless you make some adjustments to your diet and exercise regimen.

Still, it's very difficult to not gain the extra ten pounds or so. That's one of the side effects of Lyrica, potential weight gain and it could make you drowsy depending on the dosage. At the end of the day though, for the last few years, it is the medication of choice that works for me along with CBD oil, some natural supplements, massage therapy and lidocaine and ketamine infusions every couple of months.

Now, when I say these pain management methods work for me it doesn't mean they eliminate the pain entirely; instead they reduce it. They take the pain level/symptoms from say an eight out of ten, ten being the worst possible pain you can have, to a three out of ten. Better than nothing, right? Right.

The reason why I'm so conflicted every time I take Lyrica is because I have a weight gain obsession. As a child and a teenager I went through phases with my weight where I was often reminded about being too heavy. I in turn became very angry, upset, and ashamed. I didn't want to be heavy. I was an athlete, but an athlete that loved food. Question is, who doesn't love food? Let's just say there have been certain points in my life where I've loved it a little too much.

In my early teenage years what occurred far too often was I would be the guy wearing a tee shirt in the swimming pool. I'd also be too scared to change in the boy's changing room in front of all the guys for fear of negative remarks about my heaviness, so I went to a stall behind a closed door. I sucked in my belly frequently too when looking in the mirror or sometimes when posing for a picture; I still do. It's a constant battle for me, every single day. You might know the feeling too and if so, I empathize with you.

The thing is, the pain I have on the daily, I didn't even know existed, until it arrived. An invisible chronic injury that developed to my neurological system, in doctor's terms, called peripheral neuropathy or simply put, neuropathy. Small fiber nerve damage underneath the feet is what I struggle with most along with some lingering dull nerve pain down my right leg. I'm being tested for all this at a hospital in Toronto to find out if there is any kind of chance that this condition might be reversible. I've tried everything except surgery, which doesn't seem like a promising road. Currently there is "no known cure" for peripheral neuropathy. I have to hope for a miracle.

Otherwise it's try and mask the symptoms daily for life? Maybe. Hey, speaking of miracles, life is a miracle, right? I think it is. My brother reminds me that it is often. I agree. Life is what we make it.

Describing the physical pain I go through daily is quite simple; Imagine walking on crushed cereal with your shoes on, with every step you take, and then every so often it changes to pins and needles and shooting pain. At night time if I'm away from the house and walking somewhere, whether it's from work to the subway and then to my car, the pain often changes to burning sensations underneath and on top of my feet, especially in the summer time.

Another way of comprehending what many people who battle neuropathy go through every day is picturing this: You're at the beach and you're just about to leave to go home, but you have that leftover sand on the bottom of your feet and the fountain to rinse your feet off is too far. So you slip your shoes on and walk to your car despite being uncomfortable. That's it. Your shoes are on and you go. Next, the feeling of sand at the bottom of your feet with your shoes on. Annoying, right? You might start thinking to yourself, *Ok, well, the fountain to rinse my feet off wasn't that far. I should have gone.*

Well, with chronic everyday neuropathy you can't say "I should have gone." The sand would be in your shoes every day. Then, once you've just about had it with the sand and you're just so fed up, that's when all the other symptoms mentioned above start to take over by taking their turns throughout the day. That's what chronic neuropathy is—in the lower extremities anyway.

Do I exaggerate my neuropathy pain? Not in the slightest. Some might think I do, but if you're the one going through it, you know you're not. Granted, some days are better than others, but for folks that struggle with it, they're not making up this invisible pain they're feeling each and every day. Do you take more medication to try and control the symptoms as time goes on because you're so sick of it?

Certainly—at least I do anyway. For some, maybe not. Some people's pain tolerances are much higher than others.

What I find helps distract from the pain is trying to live in the moment as much as possible, as well as taking the mind-over-matter approach. Worrying about what you can control rather than what you can't, practicing gratitude often, and involving yourself in daily meditation are also helpful tools for those trying to cope with chronic pain. I will say this, medication is currently helping me live in the moment more effectively. Hopefully it continues to work.

If the pain can be managed, it's better than nothing. And remember, just like my uncle preaches: pain is inevitable, suffering is optional. I'm going to do everything in my power to try and not suffer. More life. Less pain. Live well.

3

ANTI-SEMITISM IN AMERICA

"Robbie, don't forget to send your applications out for university or college." That was said quite frequently by teachers and guidance counsellors in my last year of high school. Only thing was, I knew there was no way I was going to accept second best. What do I mean by that? I didn't want to attend a Canadian university or college the September after high school graduation took place in June. I was eighteen years old at the time and I thought to myself: If I can't make it as a Major League Baseball player, my last dream surrounding playing the game of baseball is to somehow be able to obtain a baseball scholarship in the U.S. and play college baseball in the United States of America.

When you have a vision about something, you need to remain focused on it, and though it may take some time, never lose sight of that vision. Be persistent in your quest. I knew this was going to take time, so I studied up on it. I went to a book store and grabbed the biggest book you could find on how to obtain a scholarship in the United States of America. It had everything from information on academic scholarships to all kinds of sports scholarships. The process is like applying for a job, if you're G-d's gift to baseball, which I wasn't, it's not. You see, back in 2001, most schools that offered a baseball program in America offered less than twelve full scholarships per year. Less than twelve! With anywhere between thirty and forty players on a team, that wasn't very much. I had to work for this dream and I had to work hard.

I was invited out to several training camps at universities and colleges in the U.S. It was a way for coaches to see how you played in person. A lot of potential student-athletes were from out of town, so it was a smart way to go about business on their part. Only thing was, with all those invites and being from Canada, I needed quite a bit of money to travel from town to town in the United States trying to impress coaches. I didn't have "quite a bit of money." I was eighteen years old and hadn't even graduated high school yet. I needed to find another way to stay top of mind to the coaches.

A former Major League Baseball player that I was able to get in contact with owned a baseball facility in Newmarket, Ontario that helped people like me achieve their college baseball dreams! I was so relieved. Thankfully this wasn't going to be as tricky as I first thought. What would happen is, you would make a baseball demo with him at his indoor baseball facility and when you were proud of it, you'd send it off to coaches and schools in the U.S. hoping to receive one of those full baseball scholarships. It really was like trying to win the lottery, for me anyway. So many talented baseball players out there, yet not so much scholarship money to be offered. You had to take the chance on investing in your talent though if you wanted it bad enough, which I did. We showcased my hitting and infield skills on the video. I was mostly a second baseman during my playing days. The video, which was on VHS by the way (I know, what's that?), was ready to be sent off to the United States.

It took a while for the video to really catch someone's attention. Eventually it did and I received feedback, but no scholarship offers. Some invites to training camp were on the table, but again, not one single offer. I knew I was good enough to play college baseball in the United States. I just wasn't sure if the scholarship was going to be made available to me, until one day when I got a different kind of invite. I was invited to a college fair that would take place in downtown Toronto with a few recruiters from schools in the U.S. that were going to be in attendance. The recruiters were going to be discussing scholarships. Of course I was going to attend! How could I not? I RSVPed, made an appointment with a recruiter, and put the date in my agenda. At last! Something to look forward to.

The recruiter was an older man, grey hair, and glasses. He was also wearing a sports jacket with a dress shirt underneath and jeans with a nice pair of shoes the day that I met him in downtown Toronto. We shook hands and I recall being super nervous throughout our conversation. He revealed some information on the baseball scholarship program at the school, which sounded fantastic. The way they had handled things from a scholarship stand point made a lot of sense for people like me. What do I mean by that? Well, to be quite honest with you, I was good at baseball, but I was never G-d's gift to the game.

So, I knew the likelihood of receiving a full baseball scholarship would be slim, but I was still hopeful there'd be a place for guys like me at the college level in the U.S. Thankfully this was one of those places.

I'll refrain from writing the name of the university I'm referring to, but I will tell you the university was located in the state of Iowa. In case you didn't know, saying "college" and "university" means the same thing in the United States. There's no difference (for my Canadian friends). After speaking with the recruiter, I learned that this university wasn't going to offer me a full baseball scholarship but instead a partial one. That's ok, right? It still would equal dream fulfillment.

Turns out it was the best offer I would get. The recruiter told me they tended to do that most of the time. You know, spread the wealth somewhat evenly amongst the baseball players instead of handing out full rides. This was also an NAIA Division II school, so the rules were slightly different from the NCAA in terms of how scholarships were handed out. The NCAA stands for the "National Collegiate Athletic Association" and the NAIA stands for the "National Association of Intercollegiate Athletics." The NCAA is the more prestigious league at the college level in the U.S., but being in the NAIA is still great too.

At the end of the day it was always about playing college baseball in the United States for me. It didn't matter which level, league, division, or school. I tried to keep my eye on the prize. What really made me want to say yes to the offer from the recruiter and the school right off the bat was that they were willing to accept some of my tuition money in Canadian funds. This was back in 2002, so with how horrible the Canadian dollar was next to the American back then, I really appreciated that.

Before the recruiter left for the day, I asked him what it meant when the school stated it was sponsored by the community of Christ. Being Jewish and growing up in a primarily Jewish town for most of my life, this became concerning. Would I feel rejected? Would I be accepted? Would there be anyone else attending the school that didn't practice what is preached through the community of Christ? As you can probably tell, my mind was racing. Then the recruiter eased my anxiety and told me that everyone of all faiths and ethnicities were accepted and welcome at the school.

Fantastic! I thought. I shook his hand again, took the paperwork that he had for me and then thanked him for the information and appointment. I told him that I'd think my decision over that night and discuss it with my parents before possibly signing off on the deal officially and faxing over the paperwork. He smiled, as did I and off I went. Deep breaths on the subway ride home. I was excited. I just KNEW I had to do this.

It was very difficult to convince Mom and Dad that this was the right move for me. In their eyes I was their little boy and moving out at eighteen years old was a little too soon for them. I understood, but not fully because I wasn't in their shoes. I felt bad and didn't want to upset them but at the same time this was my dream and when Robbie Shatzky gets something in his mind like this, it's difficult to persuade him not to go after it. The pleading continued and continued until finally my mom and dad were on board. What a relief. I gave them the biggest hug ever and thanked them for their support.

January 2002 arrived and I had a flight booked to Kansas City, Missouri. KCI was the closest airport that bordered the school I was about to attend in Iowa. My parents dropped me off at the airport in Toronto and we said so long. The semester was going to be about four months in length, so I'd see them again at the end of May.

When I boarded the plane, I realized it was the first time I had been on one since I was about three years old when going to Miami with my mom. I sat back, tried to close my eyes, and did my best to remain calm. The next thing I knew we were up in the air and then we landed. It felt very quick. Luckily it was a direct flight that was about two hours long. I can't quite remember who picked me up at the airport in Kansas City, but I do know it was a rep from the university.

It took two hours to drive to the school. We were surrounded by dead corn fields and grain bins on the way there. Saw a few farm animals too, mostly cows. I knew what I was in for though. The school was in the middle of nowhere. A welcomed change from the big city. When we arrived, I met up with the recruiter, who showed me around campus. It was nice. Very well kept, especially all the sports facilities. I was very impressed. The baseball field was off-campus, which I would head out and see later in the day, and when I laid eyes on the indoor basketball facility on campus, I couldn't believe how massive it was. In the winter it would turn out to be our indoor space for baseball practice and running—when the basketball team wasn't using it of course.

My mouth dropped when I saw the soccer and football fields, they were incredibly well taken care of. There wasn't one piece of grass out of place. That was one of the reasons I wanted to play baseball in the States, because I was fascinated with the playing surfaces at most fields. I can't even begin to tell you how nice and well-kept they are next to ours in Canada. You may have seen this for yourself and I'm not knocking the country that I'm so very proud to live in. It's just the U.S. cares a little more about their sports facilities, and as an athlete I took note of that. When the tour wrapped up, I looked out at the American flag blowing in the wind a top of the school and it was at that moment a tear rolled down my cheek and I knew I was exactly where I was supposed to be.

Here's how transportation worked in order to get to our home baseball field from school; Some days consisted of a few of my fellow teammates driving us in the back of their pick-up trucks. Not sure if that was allowed back then in Iowa? But I thought, *Sure. What the hell, why not?* Mostly everyone else was doing it.

We sat there and there were no real seats. It was just that, the back of a pick-up truck. You know you're in rural Iowa then. Don't think you would ever see that in big cities such as Toronto or New York. Mind you, we were a five-minute drive to the field from the school so we weren't taking a chance for very long, but still, it was a chance nonetheless. Sometimes a few of us would walk from school to the field for practice or home games. Depended who wanted to or not. It was about a twenty-minute walk, but on that first visit to the field it was neither of those methods. Instead, I was driven to the ballpark by the recruiter in a regular, everyday kind of vehicle.

We got out of the car and walked towards the ballpark. I was introduced to the head coach and was then briefed on how the baseball schedule would align with my academics. I was informed that my uniform and practice attire would be ready in the athletic center on campus the next day. *Cool,* I thought. I couldn't wait to try on my new college threads. The recruiter and I ended up watching the guys practice for a bit and then headed back to campus. It had been a long day. I was ready to unpack and go to bed.

I lived in a dorm room on campus and my roommate was from Fort Worth, Texas. He had pictures of Marines all over the wall. He wanted to be one. I found that to be very respectable. What didn't I find respectable? The fact that he had a pet tarantula. Yes, I lived in the same room as a tarantula for a couple of months. You know the saying "sleep with one eye open"? Oh, trust me, for the first couple of nights I did.

How did I get to sleep after that? Well, I actually confronted my roommate to let him know that I didn't feel comfortable with the spider in the room even though the poison had been taken out of it. He assured me that the aquarium it was in was secure and it had been caged off at the top so it would not be able to escape unless we opened the gate of the cage at the top to allow it. That news helped me sleep at night, but you can still be certain that I had a nightmare or two that consisted of me waking up with that thing on my face. I'm grateful that those nightmares never became a reality.

The first week in the dorms was all about trying to get to know who my neighbors were. So, I introduced myself to some of my peers that were living in several other dorm rooms on my floor. One guy named Christopher was very passionate about trying to get to the bottom of the 9/11 tragedy. He had articles and pictures of the planes hitting the towers all over his room. It almost looked and felt like he was investigating the tragic outcome. Then there was a fellow from Pensacola, Florida studying to become a priest.

I thought, *Why would you go to a school all the way in Iowa when you were from Florida?* There were so many schools in Florida, plus it was way nicer weather wise. I guess it was cheaper here? Maybe. Oh, and by the way, the same could have been asked of me too. Why would a guy that spent all of his eighteen years on this planet in the New York City of Canada move all the way out to rural Iowa for his education? I can't exactly remember what his answer was when I asked him, and mine as you know was to chase a dream. Turns out I'd become pretty close friends with that guy from Florida during my stay in Iowa. His name was Josh. The dorm room to my right was occupied by Jesus (Hey-soose).

He was my teammate, originally from Arizona and recruited as our team's shortstop. The railings on the side of his bed were filled with plastic spit cups. The spit was mixed with tobacco. He chewed tobacco like there was no tomorrow. I don't think there was ever a time I saw him not chewing tobacco. At least one of his cheeks was puffy all the time. The plastic spit cup situation in his room was incredibly gross to me. It wasn't very sanitary either. I couldn't have been the only one to acknowledge that when passing by his room. Thank goodness he wasn't my roommate. I was beginning to think that living with a tarantula wasn't so bad after all.

When you left the dorm room hallway to leave the building there was a cross on the wall, or at least I thought there was. It kind of looked like two swords clashing in the middle and if my memory serves me correctly there were a couple of horses painted on the wall too. Every time I walked by it, I questioned whether or not it was a cross. I had always attended public schools growing up, so I was just curious. It didn't matter to me because I would respect it either way. I was told I'd be accepted for who I was, so I was going to accept the school for who they were.

On a slightly cool, early morning with the sun shining, I walked across campus staring out at the American flag on top of the school blowing in the wind. Again, I was reminded of how lucky I was. I made sure to stare out at that flag for a few seconds every day I was there. We were about to board the bus to play a road game in Missouri and it turned out we weren't stepping foot into an actual bus but rather travel vans. That happened sometimes when a bus wasn't available to take us. I ducked my head and stepped into one of the vans to find out there weren't enough actual seats in the vans for everyone, so I traveled the entire way sitting on the floor next to the sliding door of the van. Each road trip was about two to three hours one way. That's a long time to be sitting on the floor.

In the States, it works like this. Freshman, sophomore, junior, and then senior. Those were your four years of college. Freshmen normally got treated like an intern at a company would, which is not usually the greatest and perhaps worse in terms of your duties. We were the odd men out when it came to actually sitting in seats in travel vans when there was no space.

On game and practice days we were also the ones assigned to carry the equipment to and from the field. And on really rainy days that occurred on game days, we'd be the ones to get an early phone call from Coach explaining why we should head on out to the field early. It usually meant we were to collect the accumulating water from the rain that had fallen on the field overnight and that we should put it in buckets and empty them out. We essentially tried to make the field playable even though it was raining, and then some of us, if not most of us, freshmen wouldn't even see an inning of play during the game.

Remember, there were thirty guys on the team, nine starters. It's very difficult to see playing time in your first year. It's possible, but your playing abilities really need to stand out amongst the rest. I wasn't quite there yet. I was also injured. I had been trying to rehab a small broken bone that was floating in my right elbow, which just so happened to be my throwing arm. Back to the task at hand though, stretching and warming up. We had arrived at the ballpark.

Central Missouri State University, I couldn't believe we were playing there. The ballpark was magnificent. Almost comparable to a Minor League Stadium. It had real dugouts and stadium seats that looked like it could hold up to at least one thousand fans. Incredible. The field was ready and it was time to play ball! Halfway through the game, our ace walked by me in the dugout. "Ace" if you didn't know, stands for a star pitcher in baseball lingo. He said to me in a loud voice so everyone else on the team could hear, "Hey Shatzky. What kind of last name is Shatzky? Is that Jewish? Are you Jewish Shatzky!"

Instantly I felt a lump in my throat. Someone certainly knew how to catch me off guard. Especially the way he asked me that. "Are you Jewish Shatzky?" Almost like he had never met another Jewish person in his life. Maybe he hadn't. My palms began to sweat. I was actually quite startled. What would my teammates do if they found out I was Jewish?

I was certainly a minority at the school. There was one other Jewish person that attended the same school and she was half Jewish. I did the research though; I knew Jewish people weren't liked very much over the years in certain parts of the world, but I wasn't about to deny who I was, what I was born into. I was, and still am, very proud to be Jewish. So, in response to our ace I said, "Yes. Yes, I am Jewish."

Some of my teammates on the bench turned their heads towards me, their jaws dropped and one of them said, "Really! Are you serious? You're Jewish Shatzky?" I was obviously from outer space with the looks they were giving me at this point. I could feel my face turning red and a knot in my stomach starting to form.

"Yes, I'm Jewish," I responded.

Our ace proceeded to say, "I figured you were Jewish with that kind of last name." All of a sudden, a ball had been hit into play distracting from the awkwardness of the scenario I was put in. That ended up being the third out of the inning. Next thing you know my teammates ran out onto the field to go and play defense and I was left on the bench to try and digest what had just happened.

I didn't mind carrying the baseball bags to and from the field. I was a rookie and was just glad that I was part of a college baseball team in the United States of America. That being said, there is a fine line you don't cross when it comes to talking to your teammates, and what was about to take place made me not only not want to carry the team baseball bags ever again but it also made me feel like I could no longer trust my "teammates." And that was huge. It's about respect and it's not just a one-way street.

At practice one day after stretching, I walked over to one of my teammates and asked if he wanted to throw the ball around. He responded with a question, "Hey Shatzky, are you still Jewish?" and then he laughed.

The laughter got louder when another teammate walked by us and sarcastically responded to the question for me. He said, "Oh, no, I'm not Jewish anymore. I converted." Then they both laughed together. My palms started to sweat again.

What was going on here? This behavior was unacceptable. Was it anti-Semitic? At that point I wasn't sure, but I could tell they were picking on me. I get the whole being picked on for being a rookie, but don't include my religion with it. I barely knew them. Couldn't they tell they were crossing the line with what they were saying? Obviously not. I tried my best to suck it up and keep my head held high, but, on the inside, I couldn't come to grips with my reality. I was scared of my teammates.

Did I feel accepted? Absolutely not. Their behavior was very much concerning, and I was beginning to wonder how much more I could tolerate. Realistically I should have stood up for myself instantly and not tolerated any of it. I think I was just too shocked to say anything. It was a period where I was in disbelief that this was actually happening to me. Kind of like my dream was getting turned upside down and I didn't want to believe it. This was the last thing I had expected. From that moment on, carrying the baseball equipment around that belonged to the team became more and more like a chore. I thought to myself, *Why should I help them while they joke around about me being Jewish?*

It wasn't every single one of my teammates rubbing me the wrong way, but still, I was conflicted.

Unfortunately, the small-minded behavior continued. To try and combat it and take my mind off things I ended up on a road trip over spring break with a few friends from school. I needed the mental break. I think we all do when we get to a certain point in our busy lives. A couple of vehicles were rented and off we went. We drove all the way from Iowa to Dallas, Texas and then from Dallas to Brownsville, Texas. Brownsville borders Matamoras, Mexico. We crossed the border into Matamoras for one day and I recall seeing an injured dog limping, a lot of garbage piled up on neighborhood streets, and what almost looked like prison bars would be at the end of several driveways in hopes to keep vehicles secure.

It was obvious that there was a lot of theft to be concerned about in that part of Mexico. In total, we drove about thirty-five hours over the course of ten days. Most of our time however, was spent in Brownsville. It was very Americanized. We did a lot of sight-seeing on our trip and spent some time at the beach.

I actually met a girl in Texas and when I came back to the field for practice after spring break, I told my teammates about her while we were getting our stretches in on the grass. One of my teammates —I can't quite remember his name, we'll call him John—then looked over to me and in front of everyone said, "Hey Shatzky, did you fuck her through a blanket?"

Instantly laughter occurred.

I then laughed it off as well to pretend like I had a good attitude about what was just said even though I wasn't sure what he meant. I never answered the question and I made some google searches when I got back to campus. He was referring to the mistaken belief regarding sexual relations of Ultra-Orthodox Jews.

This was the turning point for me. I was fully coherent and knew that my life and my dream was being tarnished by anti-Semitic remarks. I found it very difficult to deal with. My emotions were everywhere. Remember, I was only 18. This was the first time I left the nest. I missed Mom and Dad a lot. I missed my brother. The bottom line was, I was getting very overwhelmed and started to feel really lonely way out in the Midwest in a town of about 3,500 people. The sun began to set as I looked out my dorm room window. More grain bins and more farm animals. I didn't mind. The state of Iowa itself seemed quite peaceful, but I was disgusted, shocked, and in disbelief with all the ignorance.

When walking to class one day I bumped into a friend of mine. He was the only black player on the school's basketball team. I told him about my situation briefly and asked if he had experienced any racism on campus or from his teammates because well, let's face it, we were both minorities in this part of the U.S. He said he did. I told him I thought that was horrible and that he should never have to experience anything like that. I could tell he appreciated my support. We agreed that we'd both try and hang in there and stay positive. We also wished one another luck with our academics and off we were going about the day. I never did end up hearing much from him again after that run in and I sure hope life has been treating him well.

The travel vans were packed and ready to go. I walked back over to campus to meet up with my teammates and to be briefed by our head coach. A long drive and a few out of state games in Arkansas meant we'd be staying in a hotel for a couple days. I can't quite remember if I had a seat to myself in the van the whole way. I think part of the way I got to sit down on a cushioned seat. Lucky me! Didn't happen much for the rookies like I said. So, when it did, we were appreciative. It was after dark by the time we had arrived, and everyone was tired. Specific curfew times weren't really the norm, but as long as we made sure to try and get to bed at a decent time the night before a game, Coach was ok with that.

We checked into the hotel, and before getting some shut eye I made sure to polish my cleats. This was something Coach made a requirement for all of us on the team. He wanted us to show up looking sharp and professional on game days, similar to big leaguers. We were also never allowed much facial hair, one to two days' stubble at most. That reminded me, I had to shave in the morning. I thought to myself, *Maybe I'll get it out of the way now and just shave?* Nah, I was too tired. It had been a long day. Time for bed.

The sky was blue and the sun was shining the next day in Batesville, Arkansas—perfect baseball weather. I still hadn't seen an inning of college baseball. To be honest with you, I was injured, so I red-shirted the semester, which meant I saved a year of my playing eligibility at the collegiate level. I played in scrimmage games and faced college pitching in the states, but I hadn't played in a real game. My polished cleats were extra shiny that day with the sun glistening from above. Social media hadn't been invented at that point but I wanted to have my picture taken in my uniform, just for keep sake.

Wearing my clean baseball uniform, with my batting gloves and bat in hand, I was ready to pose. One of my teammates snapped the photo. It's developed and laying around somewhere in my parent's house. Hopefully I can find it again. It's been eighteen years. Our team won that day so everyone was in a good mood. As we left the diamond, we all walked along the first baseline on the outskirt of the playing field towards the parking lot. All of a sudden, I looked up and noticed a full moon in the sky during the daytime. The sky was still royal blue and the moon was out at the same time the sun had been.

Odd, I thought. It's not every day you see that happen. I mentioned it to some of my teammates on our walk to the parking lot. I sounded a bit excited about it and was then made fun of by one of my teammates for mentioning something they thought wasn't that odd. I was surprised that I was being made fun of at that moment and that's probably why I didn't stick up for myself. I didn't know what to say because I was caught so off guard. "Leave the guy alone!" one of my other teammates quipped back. At last, someone was actually standing up for me and it felt good.

His name was Rocco and it's been great to reconnect with him again online eighteen years after we last played baseball together. I made sure to thank him again for sticking up for me all those years ago. Next stop, the hotel.

Laughter erupted while beer bottles were being passed around amongst my teammates in celebration of our big victory earlier that day. I was happy to see the guys so stoked, but that happiness quickly faded. The laughter grew louder in the hotel room and that's when one of my teammates, who'd heard me talk about the sun and the moon being out at the same time earlier, yelled out over top of the noise, "Hey guys, not only is Shatzky a dumb ass, but he's a fucking Jewish bastard too!"

There was instant laughter to that remark from everyone in the room but me. The laughter began to get really obnoxious. You know when you use the term "laugh out loud" but you're not really laughing out loud? These guys were literally laughing out loud, and they were laughing so hard too. I stood there in disbelief trying to hide my real feelings. I smiled like everything was ok, but I knew it wasn't. Where was I? Was this still Planet Earth?

The drinks continued to flow; everyone was partying, but not me of course. All I could think of doing next was leaving that hotel room. I was disgusted, felt nauseous, and my palms were really sweaty. All symptoms of anxiety. How could I leave the party without making it obvious that I was emotionally scarred by what just happened? Eventually I escaped and I think it was because I had to use the bathroom and the one in the hotel room we were all gathered in was occupied.

One of my teammates asked where I was going and I told him I was going to find another restroom. I ended up finding a bathroom and never returned to the party. I didn't even say goodnight to the guys. Did they care? Probably not. I went back to my room. Tears began to run down my face. I was so far from home. Close to a sixteen-hour drive actually. What was I going to do? I was hoping that this was all just some kind of nightmare and that I'd eventually wake up and all would be ok. But that's the thing, it wasn't. My dream had actually been turned into a nightmare and I felt lonely to top it off.

My parents didn't know about any of the anti-Semitic remarks and behavior because I didn't want to scare them. I also didn't want them to encourage me to come home because of it. This put me over the edge though. It was about time I spoke to Mom and Dad and let them know what was really happening to their eighteen-year-old son. I just couldn't take it anymore.

I was done.

My guidance counsellor shut the door to her office. "Have a seat," she said.

I complied. It was a sunny, cool, crisp morning in Iowa that day. The sun beamed into her office through the blinds that weren't entirely closed. I began to squint. "So, Robbie, how do you want to handle this?" she asked.

I automatically thought to myself, *So I guess the ball is fully in my court?* Wasn't the school going to be the ones to help me do something about all this? Maybe not. I sat there thinking with my chin on my fist. "I'd like to speak with them," I said. "These guys need to know what they are saying is unacceptable. They need to be put in their place and be taught a verbal lesson. All I need is about ten minutes of their time. All thirty of them. I'll write down what needs to be said and we'll go from there."

She replied, "Alright, I'll get your coach up to speed." I thanked her for her time and off I went. It was time to come up with one of the most impactful speeches of my life.

Upon arrival to the ballpark I noticed my teammates sitting up against the fence. All thirty of them. This wasn't the norm. Usually they would have been warming up by now, or at least stretching. I began to get nervous. My time to say something was about to come.

Coach opened with a brief introductory speech in front of all of us, explaining a little bit about what I had been going through during the semester and shamed some of my teammates in the process for being so ignorant and inconsiderate. Coach often had a way with words that made you know he was upset. He was tough, but fair. He was the kind of coach that made you run from foul pole to foul pole over and over again at the baseball field if you had failing grades. Not only did he want for you to have a great work ethic on the field, but in the classroom too.

The stage had been set; it was my turn to say what I had to say. To sum it up, I let my teammates know I was really hurt by all the remarks, that I worked incredibly hard to get where I was at with baseball and that they ruined my dream. I reminded them that I was a rookie, that I picked up after them, I carried their bags and became part of the grounds crew at times, just so they could play in a game, while I watched on the bench. "That's how you treat me? With those anti-Semitic remarks?" I said.

I carried on by saying, "We aren't in the 1960's anymore and I'm astonished that this type of behavior is still taking place." Most of all, I told them I was finally speaking up on behalf of whomever that next student might be to arrive in town with the same or similar dream of playing college ball. You know, the one that might seem like a little bit of an outcast or minority. I said, "I hope that he or she would never have to face the torment that I have as a student/athlete here." The speech concluded and then there was a few seconds of silence.

It felt like the weight of the world had been lifted off my shoulders. At last, I stood up for myself. The guys who should have apologized to me came over to apologize before beginning their warmups. Most of the apologies seemed authentic and heartfelt. One was not and still very ignorant. The authentic and heartfelt ones went something like this, "Robbie, I'm very sorry. I shouldn't have said what I said. I feel really bad about it."

And the ignorant one? He said, "I'm sorry Robbie, I didn't know my comments would have offended you." It's like, duh, how could you not know that?

For what they were worth, I accepted each and every apology regardless of whether or not they actually meant it, and if what I said in my speech in front of all my teammates actually made those ball players think twice about the next time they were going to open their mouth and say something racist to someone and then not actually go through with it, then speaking up was the right thing for me to do. Maybe I made a difference? I sure hope so, but truthfully, I'll never know.

There is a synagogue in Pittsburgh, PA that is sadly the site where the deadliest attack ever on the Jewish community in the U.S. occurred. One day I hope to make it out there and pay my respects to the innocent lives taken back in October of 2018. Now, although

I can't fully understand what those families of the victims have gone through and continue to go through daily, I can relate to some degree. It's about feeling hatred for being Jewish and feeling hatred towards how you were raised. It's unfortunate that some people can't see the beauty in the differences we have in our world. Just because two people don't agree on something doesn't mean you have to despise one another. If everyone were raised the same or had the same opinion, how boring would our world be?

Very boring.

Religion comes down to preference. It's about what you choose to believe in. Acceptance and cheering for one another, despite their race, sexuality, gender, origin, and color of skin is what it should be all about and what we should strive for in this world. That's the key to a more peaceful and prosperous future for everyone. In the meantime, I will continue to pray for the families and friends of those whose lives were innocently taken foolishly and disgustingly by a gunman in Pittsburgh on that Shabbat morning in late October 2018.

Mom was right. I never did return to that university in Iowa in the fall. I actually never returned again. Even though the guys had apologized, I just didn't feel the same anymore. I couldn't get over the fact that I was still disgusted with what had happened in my first semester. I was turned off. When you feel that way, it's difficult to return to a place that doesn't make you feel good inside.

The entire situation as a whole left an emotional scar with me that I don't think will ever go away. Hence me writing about it eighteen years after the fact. I was also injured a lot and it was time for me to get serious about what I was going to do with my life after baseball. I like to think that I still fulfilled my dream though in all this, which if you think about it, I did. As I've told you before, the dream itself was to obtain a baseball scholarship in the U.S. and to play college baseball there. Both bucket list items had thankfully been checked off.

What else would I have liked to have happen? Well, similar to one of the characters in my favorite baseball movie, I never got an at bat in a real college baseball game in the U.S. That would have been nice too. Realistically, the main problem in all this was that the experience didn't pan out the way I would have liked it to. Listen, shit happens sometimes. Some of it can be out of our control and a lot of the time we might not get everything we want. The key is to find a happy medium and to stay as grounded and positive as possible no matter what kind of curve ball gets thrown in our direction. Oh, and never be afraid to speak up when you don't feel respected. Life goes on and despite what happened, I still very much love the game of baseball, hopefully you do too.

4

MARILENA

You know those people that skate around at a recreational skate in what would usually be a yellow jacket and marked "Skate Patrol"? The ones that say, "Excuse me, you can't be skating backwards"? Ya, that was me.

I can't tell you how much I loved that job growing up. Skating is a passion of mine, so it made sense. I volunteered when I was 15 and worked skate patrol from 16-19 years of age. Thankfully I stuck around in my last year because, had I not, I might not have met my incredible wife Marilena. While I worked skate patrol at a few local rinks nearby my parent's home, Marilena worked as a receptionist at one of the recreation centers I worked at for skate patrol. Not only that but I would workout at the gym in one of those recreation centers.

One day after finishing up a workout, a guy named Gary walked out of the gym with me. Let's just say Gary liked to schmooze. He was the gossip king of the gym. Always wanting to know what people were up to, who they were dating, etc. As we were walking towards the front reception area, he said, "Bye," to the lady that was working behind the desk. I waved bye too.

Gary asked me how my workout was, I asked how his was, and

once we arrived in the parking lot about to say bye to one another, he mentioned the woman who was working behind the front desk.

He said something like, "That woman we just saw, she's really good looking, eh?"

I smiled, turned red, and agreed with him.

Gary went on to say, "Her name is Marilena. You know, she has a thing for you."

I reacted very shy like. I said, "You can't be serious. She likes *me*?"

Gary replied, "Yup. You better ask her out before I do."

To which I then responded, "Let's not let that happen." Gary must have been in his early 50s at the time and Marilena was in her early 20s. I told Gary I was going to work up the courage to ask her out.

Thankfully Marilena said, "Yes," when I asked her out on a date. Gary was so happy to have played matchmaker. Our first date was an interesting one to say the least. I don't know where I got the weird idea of walking through a park with Marilena at nighttime and showing her what looked to be like a haunted house and really old graveyard that I knew of, but that's what occurred.

I took a chance. I wanted us to live on the edge a little. Our hearts were racing and we seemed to enjoy the thrill—at least I did anyway. Luckily she didn't want to not continue on with the date as we went to Starbucks for hot chocolate afterwards. Marilena went to the bathroom as I stood in line waiting to order the drinks. As soon as she stepped out of the bathroom I began walking towards her with a tray with our orders on it. Two medium hot chocolates which quickly became no more, not because we drank them but because I tripped, lost my footing and spilled both drinks all over the floor.

Embarrassing right?

Very.

It was our first date. I totally thought that would have been the end for me with Marilena, but it wasn't. She obviously looked beyond my klutzy moment, and weird first date locations to give me another chance, and another chance would eventually come. Let's just say the rest is history.

I think what I appreciate most about Marilena is her selflessness. She really impressed me by travelling around Canada with me so I could fulfill some of the most meaningful work dreams that I've ever had. That literally meant the world to me. Not every partner out there would be that supportive and she deserves every bit of credit putting up with me along the way. Also just in general, Marilena is a selfless person, often putting others before her and she'd do just about absolutely anything for her family. It's admirable.

Back in 2013/2014, also known as the leadup to Madison's birth, Marilena went through a treacherous pregnancy. What was supposed to be a mostly happy time ended up being a nightmare for Marilena. The pregnancy made her very ill. Our house turned into a makeshift hospital. Nurses were visiting twice daily to administer the medication Marilena needed in order to keep her and our baby alive. Knowing Marilena though, I can tell you she is quite the fighter and thankfully she made it to the finish line of her pregnancy. Due to the severity of her pregnancy, she was advised by medical professionals to have a C-section. So that's what she did, and I can't tell you how grateful I am that we had a happy, healthy baby in the end.

You know how you might see several posts on social media where someone says, "Mom and baby are doing ok"? Well, the baby was, but Marilena wasn't. It took pregnancy to discover that Marilena had thyroid cancer. So, in a way Madison saved my wife's life and Madison doesn't even know it yet. She'll tell her one day when she's ready.

Marilena had to have another two surgeries, this time to remove her entire thyroid. That was a C-Section and then two thyroid surgeries four and five months after she gave birth. Once the thyroid was removed so was the cancer. Marilena still has to go for checkups every few months to make sure the cancer doesn't grow back. She also has to take a pill daily in place of no longer having a thyroid. If she doesn't take it regularly she could die. That's how important that pill is.

You might think, *Hey, hooray her thyroid is removed so the cancer is gone fully!* On one hand that's correct, but on the other it's not unfortunately. It can grow back so that's why she goes for her routine check-ups. I can't tell you how much I've learned over the last eight years or so in regards to how much the thyroid regulates in the body. Practically everything.

For example, no longer having one means Marilena feels heat about five or ten times more than the average person does. She can only tolerate so much if she's in the sun somewhere in the summer time, down south, or in a sauna, not that I think she'd ever go in a sauna because her body feels like she's in a sauna at times without actually physically being in one. So, if you're feeling heat exhaustion after half an hour on a really warm day, you can only imagine how it would feel if it was Marilena out there.

She's also more irritable because of not having her thyroid; not her fault, it's a side effect. More side effects include anxiousness, that can kick in big time at certain moments (especially when our six year old tries to push her buttons more often than not), and mood swings are also on the list of side effects of not having a thyroid.

One more for ya, she's exhausted all the time but tries to manage it every day. We're talking exhaustion like only had 4 hours of sleep kind of exhaustion. That's why she has to go to bed earlier than most adults to try and counter act that. As you can see, the thyroid is super important due to how much it regulates your bodily functions, so her not having one any longer is a real big challenge that nobody in this life deserves. I commend her for trying her best with it. One thing is for sure, she is not her diagnosis and still fights through every day at the best of her ability, which is amazing for all she's been through.

With all these challenges in life it takes communication, understanding, support, and hard work to make a marriage thrive. Nobody said it would be easy. If anything, you've most likely heard it would indeed be difficult. It is. Nothing good comes easy. Like I've said before though we control our thoughts and emotions and how we perceive things and certain situations.

So, if you think it will be difficult all the time and that marriage is horrible, it will be just that. If you keep an open mind though, that's when things begin to be more enjoyable. Think of it like this:

You have to take care of you and ultimately you have to be happy, but if you live with say the intent of always wanting to please your better half, I find that is one of the most successful ways of maintaining a strong, successful relationship. You also need to take care of your relationship.

One of my mentors says it best: "You should never stop dating your spouse."

Your vehicle needs to have oil changes in order to properly operate, correct? Think of your relationship like you would your vehicle. It needs maintenance for it to work.

A heart of gold is truly difficult to find these days. In a world where a lot of people are mostly out for themselves, Marilena is polar opposite. She cherishes her family and friends, and for that I'm grateful.

In a session once with my psychologist, I told him how Marilena wants to live close to her parents because they're getting older and she wants to do her best to take care of them when they need help.

My psychologist looked over at me and said, "That's a very special trait she has Rob."

I agreed. She's loyal, a great partner, and still finds time to maintain her independence too. I must admit, I'm quite the lucky guy. Marilena is a gem.

5

RADIO

It was the most magnificent thing in the world. A radio station had been built inside the high school I was a student at.

Wait, what!

Ya, my point exactly; I couldn't believe it either. No wonder the slogan for Vaughan Secondary School was "Turning Dreams into Action." That's all I wanted to do next!

106.3 RAV-FM (Radio at Vaughan) was the name of the radio station, which then later changed to 90.7 on the FM dial and is now known as 90.7 RAV-FM. The coolest part was this wasn't just any ordinary high school radio station, it was a radio station that was licensed! And did I mention it was on the FM dial! I was in heaven.

I had always been interested in radio and was so grateful the perfect outlet had arrived when I discovered it in grade 11. The mastermind behind it all was a guy also by the name of Rob. He was the station's original founder, and he used to be a teacher at Vaughan Secondary School. Rob was really well known in the radio industry at the time and even more so now. I remember it like it was yesterday. I was intimidated by the broadcast console when I first laid eyes on it.

I said to myself, *No way. There is no way I'm operating that contraption.*

All I want to do is talk when it comes to radio. This isn't working for me unless someone else operates that thing and all I do is the talking.

Boy oh boy did I ever have to change that attitude of mine, especially if I wanted to succeed in this industry. The more you know, the more valuable you become. It's funny, this is how life and radio collide in my world at times. I had often done that around the house too. I'd say to my wife, "There's no way I can do that."

Whether it be cooking a certain dish or putting together a desk from a furniture store. Marilena would respond, "You won't know unless you try."

I think that's a big thing in life. Even if you don't have the confidence, at least try. Don't be afraid to get your hands dirty. So, this time I tried, because I really wanted to. I dreamed of a career in media. I had a vision, a very clear one, which was to become a professional radio show host.

Have you ever heard of the saying "Love what you do and you'll never have to work a day in your life"? It's true. After 20 years of it, I'm confirming that the saying is true, no doubt. Obviously if you have to work a job you don't enjoy just to put food on the table for your family, go ahead and do it, but don't lose sight of your purpose, what you're meant to do in this life. Take the time to find your gift and eventually incorporate it in how you make your living. Even if that dream job of yours is part-time and you work elsewhere to make ends meet, that's ok too. Just don't waste the gift G-d gave you is all I'm saying.

It was officially time to put my ego aside and say, "You know what, all I have to do is learn about this broadcast console and I'm one step closer to living my dream of being a radio personality." So that's what I did, thanks to the help of my mentor Rob.

He taught me everything there was to know about that console and more. I eventually got my own radio show on the high school radio station. I was on the air a few days per week. I remember one of the most challenging things for me at the beginning was attempting to be my own person on the air. Who exactly was I? It turned out to be everyone but *me*.

I was constantly emulating some of my favorite announcers on

Toronto radio stations. Figuring out who you are exactly and how to portray yourself takes time. I eventually found myself. I think everyone does if you're willing to work at it. For me, it took a few moves to different cities in Canada, also some growing up and maturing, but hey, that's the way she goes sometimes. Life experiences help and still to this day I'm learning more about my feelings and emotions, sometimes more than ever before, and that is what counts most. Talking *real* life and being authentic on the air, online, and in person.

Watching my levels on the broadcast console was something Rob reminded me of often. Levels, meaning how my voice sounded in comparison to the music. The voice should always be a smidge higher than the music and on certain consoles you never want your levels to go in the red zone, or on some other consoles, past a certain number. When that occurs it would most likely pull the trigger on a clipping sound on-air. That clipping sound is a type of distortion. You don't want that to happen; it's a terrible static type of sound that you and the listener would both hear for however long you're distorting for.

As time went on, I realized just how important level watching was, and Rob would never let me forget it. Certainly, a good thing. I have thanked him for those reminders over the years. It really meant a lot to me.

When I graduated high school, that's when I hit the pause button on radio and moved to the States on that baseball scholarship I told you about. When that stint didn't work out the way I wanted it to I ended up back in Toronto kind of frustrated and unsure of what move to make next. Champions and go-getters often like to work on their next move; it's just in their blood.

I wouldn't call myself a champion, but go getter, yes, that's me, absolutely. Dreamer, that's also me and I'll touch on that some more later on. Thankfully I got some good advice from the radio contacts I had made and I ended up applying to radio broadcasting college courses in the Greater Toronto Area. When January 2003 eventually came around, that's when I started out in the radio broadcasting course at Seneca College in Toronto.

College was intimidating at first. We—and when I say we I mean the other students and I—were told that only a handful of us would make it in radio, the rest of us would wind up in something totally different in terms of a career. I knew how bad I wanted this though. I was willing to work as hard as I could for it in order to be included in that handful.

During my time as a broadcasting student in college I would often still visit the high school I graduated from. I loved the fact that the high school station was on the FM dial, the college station was not, *but* many of my college instructors worked in the radio industry, so the scenario was kind of like the best of both worlds. What also inspired me to keep working at the high school radio station was that the console was the original broadcast board from one of my favorite Toronto radio stations which just so happened to have been donated to Vaughan Secondary School with the morning show labels still stuck onto it.

Too cool! I thought.

Rob had allowed me to return to the school on Friday nights to host a three-hour show from 7-10. My friend Phil would join me to provide wrestling reports at the time. My friend Phil, or as I call him "Philly," has been there for me through a lot of the ups and downs in life, a true best friend. Most Friday nights it was a party of three in the high school. The janitor named Kevin let us in so we could get to the radio station. I fondly remember how nice he was. He always greeted us with a smile and told us he'd be listening to the show in his office when he could and sometimes, he'd even throw the station on in the school atrium.

That meant a lot. I mean, the atrium would rarely be full, but to know the station was blaring nonetheless was still an amazing feeling.

That was the thing with me though, whether it was 2 people listening or 2500 people listening, I tried my best at all times and just wanted to do the job and do it well. The motions, hitting posts before a song lyric kicked in, smiling behind the mic, greeting listeners, making them smile, entertaining, storytelling, all of it lit up my life and I was willing to give up every Friday night in my last year as a teenager in hopes to try and be one of those handful of broadcasters to make it and not have to worry about another back up plan.

It turns out I didn't think I was working enough between eight radio school courses in college and returning to my high school to volunteer once a week as a broadcaster. I still wanted more! *Bring it on,* I thought. So that's where KISS 92 came in. I interned there throughout parts of high school and college too. I also put MIX 99.9 on my resume by interning in their music department for a little while.

When I completed my one hundred hours of interning for college, which was a requirement, I decided to stay on board with KISS 92 interning and eventually catching on with part-time, paid promotional work. I was grateful for both.

It was a busy schedule but I wouldn't have had it any other way. There needed to be more though. I was always hungry for more. How could I prove to the folks who make big radio decisions that I was a young on-air talent on the rise? I had a few newspaper articles published on me, which was cool, but what else?

Finally, it hit me!

I had to send out demos to radio station program directors even though I hadn't finished school yet. Like trying to get a job before the job even existed. That way if you don't get the gig first time around, at least they know who you are by the time you finish college, and you can always send them an updated demo when you've completed school too. Establishing a connection and networking along the way, that was key. Especially the networking part, I was always reminded of it. My goal, which I reached thankfully, was to send out twenty demo tapes per semester to personnel at radio stations all across Canada, and there were four semesters in total at school.

Next thing was to make this demo. I couldn't get it out of my mind.

Now if we rewind just a bit here, the first demo came about when I was almost seventeen years old. I was just a kid. One day while interning at KISS 92 I was lucky enough to get about thirty minutes of the afternoon drive guy's time after he finished his show. He is the Canadian KING of FM radio. Been on the air for years in several markets all across Canada, so I certainly looked up to him and still do. I loved his passion for the business. Such a straight shooter. He suggested if I really wanted to make it on the air, I had to put together a really strong demo.

He wrote on a sheet of paper how I should construct that demo. I swear I remember holding on to that piece of paper like my life depended on it. I recall most of what it said too: Top of hour, intro, phone call, backsell, and weather. Essentially, you want to showcase versatility on that demo in hopes to land that first gig.

Now it was time to bring what the afternoon drive guy suggested back to the studio and try and put this thing together. Production certainly wasn't my strong suit and still isn't, so Rob back at the high school radio station was gracious enough with his time to handle the production side of it. He included all the bells and whistles in terms of the jingle package, which really made it sound like a major market demo right out of the gate. I tried to live up to the hype with the on-air presentation portion.

Having received a few critiques from some great people working in radio on the air and off, the consensus was that the demo was ready to be sent out.

Throughout college I sent demos out all over Canada. No market/audience size was too big or too small. Feedback or a gig, that was all I was after at the time. Mostly I would ask for advice. If there was a job recently posted, I'd inquire about that. My goal was to learn though. I wanted to grow and I wanted employers to be impressed with my attitude. It isn't just a saying you know, it's true. Attitude is everything. I've always taken very well to constructive criticism and I firmly believe that's what's helped me stay grounded and maintain my success not only in the radio industry but in life in general too.

Luckily, I received some email responses and telephone calls from program directors in various markets across Canada after reaching out. The program directors that I reached out to for feedback seemed at ease and at the same time surprised by the fact that new talent was knocking on their door trying to receive a critique. Most emails that were returned included constructive criticism and some compliments too. I would print and file away every single email I got back from a program director so I could re-visit them as time went on. It's all about being a student of the game!

One day I developed enough courage to ask one of the most respected broadcasters in North America if he could listen to my demo and let me know what he thought. It wasn't every day you could do something like that. Being in his class in college certainly helped because he knew I was a keener. His name was Tom. He was an on-air *legend* in the radio business, a pioneer. He lived for the job. Moved wherever needed in North America in order to succeed on the air.

It's difficult to stay married through something like that, and I imagine that contributed to his pattern of divorce and getting re-married a few times. We all make choices in life though, and those were his, not necessarily the divorces, but to live the life of a rock star and not be able to call one place home.

Throughout class, Tom would allow us to pick his brain here and there with questions about his career, the journey, and where it took him. I was hoping that he'd give me some of his time for a chat after class to tell me more and let me play him my demo. And he did. What a nice guy he was. We talked about his career; it was incredible. I don't think there was a city in North America that guy didn't work in! Exaggerating of course, but you get the idea.

It's interesting, everyone you meet in this business has a story. It's usually a unique one too, but I think Tom was one of those guys whose story topped them all. I knew we were getting towards the end of our chat and my anxiety was beginning to settle in. I was shy to ask him if he could listen to this nineteen-year-old kid's demo tape.

When I actually did build up the courage and blurted the question out, he responded not quite how I thought he would—even better than what I had imagined actually. He cared, he truly did. He said, "Let me take the tape with me and listen to it in the car a few times and I'll get back to ya."

I was hoping the end result wouldn't be that he would forget about it though. My anxiety kicked up a notch; my mind began to race. Was this scenario going to be like when I was at the ballpark as a teenager and the baseball player would say "I'll sign your ball after warming up" and then he ran into the tunnel and left me hanging? That happened sometimes believe it or not; other times it didn't. Luck of the draw I guess, and I imagine it all depends on the baseball player's mood on any given day. Hey, they're human too. It's all good.

Tom ended up keeping his word though. He pulled me aside after our next class and completely caught me off guard when he said he thought the tape sounded amazing and that he handed it to the program director at the number one most listened to FM radio station in Canada. What he said to the program director was, "This kid is ready for the big time. You told me you were looking for new, young talent, well this kid's got it."

Little did I know, right here in my own backyard, I'd be starting out professionally on the air in Toronto. I never expected this. I thought I'd start out in a small to medium sized market. Not that it mattered to me anyway. I just loved doing the job. Nevertheless, the big city was calling right out of the gate. I was nervous, I was scared, excited, anxious, you name it! I was to await a telephone call from the program director at 104.5 CHUM-FM to tell me more about hosting a weekend overnight show on CHUM-FM. All this while taking eight radio school courses during the day at school.

Some students would do something called "job out" of broadcasting school, which meant automatically getting your diploma if you found a job before graduating. That did not exist at the school I attended and I didn't want to drop out of college on my own terms. I wanted both. The diploma and the job. So, I kept to my plan. You never want to get too high or too low in this business because things change all the time. Also, I was new to Toronto airwaves so getting too confident felt a little risky.

I still couldn't believe it though. At just 19 years old I was about to be the youngest announcer to ever crack the mic on CHUM-FM. On the FM dial 104.5, it has heritage in the city of Toronto, roots and authenticity. The nerves were really starting to settle in for the first show. November 1st, 2003 from 2am-6am. I can recall showing up to the radio station at 9:30pm on Friday October 31st to begin show prepping.

When you're just starting out you're beyond eager, or at least I was. I wanted to be over prepared for the first show, plus with all the adrenaline over the last few days I was antsy to start doing my thing. The evening personality, named Taylor, was just winding down with her show when I came in and she was in a costume probably ready to head out for a Halloween party after she got off the air.

She wished me luck just before she left work and went on her way for her weekend while I was getting ready to make history? I guess you could call it that. I was about to crack the microphone at the world-famous CHUM-FM. It was only me in the studio from 2am-6am and I was quite surprised to see the request lines lighting up during those hours. It was mostly nightshift nurses calling, they couldn't believe someone was actually LIVE on the other end during their shift. The broadcast console was very familiar, as I used the older version of it in high school and was very excited to learn that the audio/editing software program we were using was VoxPro. I had used it before in college and preferred it over the others. I learned that the "next event" button was my favorite gadget in the studio. It fired off whichever song or production element that was lined up next in the music system so your mouse didn't have to. It was quick and efficient.

My first show came and went in the blink of an eye. I thought it went well. I certainly felt comfortable and confident, but not over confident. The adrenaline was still flowing. I remember taking the subway home that morning after the overnight show, and when I arrived home, I had a difficult time falling asleep. I'm already a horrible sleeper as it is, but this new schedule was totally throwing my body out of whack. I knew I couldn't complain though, this was my dream job and it just so happened to be in Canada's biggest market.

A few days passed and I ended up getting back into conversations with Rob, the program director at CHUM-FM. I was wondering what his thoughts were on the show and when I found out he loved what he heard I was incredibly thrilled. He loved it so much that he offered me more air time by adding two more overnight shows to my schedule the following weekend, which included the opportunity to be the opening act for the morning show on the Monday morning. I was so excited and overwhelmed at the same time. I couldn't believe this was all happening. *Deep breaths and one show at a time,* I told myself.

I eventually caught on with three weekend overnights throughout the remainder of the school year. It was exhausting but I still never took the schedule for granted. I was proud of my hard work and kept trying to be the best version of myself possible.

When it came time to graduate, I began to wonder what would happen with my work schedule. Was I going to stay at three overnights a week or could I do more? Three overnights eventually became five and five stayed at five, which I was good with. I mean I would have been good with three but five certainly helped out even more in terms of paying the bills and trying to set a little bit of money aside. CHUM-FM was filled with the GREATS.

Everywhere you looked along the walls were massive, world renowned artists who had visited the radio station, some of whom sat down for discussions and interviews with CHUM-FM's on-air talent. I was thrilled to now consider myself a part of that. I never actually got to interview anyone *live* on CHUM-FM, but I did get to introduce a celebrity to many of her fans in Toronto at a local area mall.

It was a long while back, and since then I've been fortunate enough to have introduced many artists on stage and at radio station promotional gatherings and events, but from what I can remember, this celebrity/artist sang and signed autographs for her fans that night.

That summer, going to bed at 8:30 on a Sunday morning after the overnight show, when the sun was rising on a very warm July day was next to impossible for me. If you love the beach and swimming pools, you probably can relate. Sundays were for the beach with family and or friends. Or at least that's what I wanted them to be at the time.

I also loved getting up in the morning to start my day the way I always had. A cup of coffee while reading a good article. You know, the small things in life. All of a sudden, my time clock was turned upside down and I somehow had to try and embrace it. But that's what we as Canadians do, right? We work hard and work to fight the good fight.

I kept reminding myself that this wasn't going to be forever and to try and thoroughly enjoy each and every show on air while I could. Let's just say I was grateful for the schedule regardless of what it was doing to my sleep cycle.

One day the afternoon drive guy from KISS 92 and I crossed paths again, this time at CHUM-FM. He was working weekends/weekday fill-in at the time for CHUM-FM while I was on overnights. He was always good at giving advice. He liked passing it down to those that cared too. He told me, "If you really want to spread your wings in this business and succeed you have to leave the city, go write your story, and then bring it back to the city." Which meant move from city to city and then if you feel inclined to do so, try and get back to Toronto. I took his advice for more reasons than one.

I was offered my first full time on-air radio job in Kitchener, Ontario. The broadcast license serves Waterloo Region, which consists of the cities Kitchener, Waterloo, and Cambridge. People in towns surrounding those cities could also hear the radio station on the FM dial and anyone else interested could listen online. I was the full-time evening show host at 91.5 THE BEAT, from 2004-2006. This is where I did the bulk of my learning in my career. I filled in on the afternoon show, mornings and live to airs. I was grateful to host some club nights throughout those couple of years too. My boss David was an incredible teacher who cared about his employees and always wanted to see them succeed.

Kitchener was also the first town I lived in on my own. I had moved out before, and lived in a dorm room with a roommate, but this time it was the real deal. I had to do everything on my own. Pay rent, pay the bills, cook for myself, do laundry, go grocery shopping, and clean my own apartment. I felt all grown up at the age of twenty. I liked it though. I've always enjoyed some independence.

What was really funny about my first apartment in Kitchener, which just so happened to be my first apartment ever, was that I had a throne for a toilet. That's right, the toilet was elevated in the bathroom. One step, two steps, three, then you were able to stand, but due to my height I'd crouch when having to go pee. I was alright with the first apartment but I wasn't completely happy with it. What I learned the hard way was that when you live in a basement, you're subject to more creepy crawlers. I lost track of the amount of times I saw centipede after centipede, and it was worse when there was a flood one time in the basement.

For an extra $50 a month I moved into a one-bedroom apartment in my second year in Kitchener. It was in a new complex. The appliances were shiny and new, the floor was clean and there was less carpet. I was content.

Waterloo Region is an amazing, vibrant part of Canada, a lot of students live there too but when I had my chance to fill in on mornings at the BEAT and the job was offered to me, I ended up passing up on it. You know when something just doesn't feel right? Something in the pit of your stomach? That was this opportunity. The co-host was a great person and all but it's real difficult to tell two people to just go do a show together and expect greatness. Sometimes that happens, but a lot of the time it doesn't.

That's why good morning shows should be cherished and never turfed. I believe everyone who works hard in this business should never be turfed, but sadly I don't control that and it's highly unlikely that happens. Especially if you're working for a big company.

I went back to evenings, but something felt off. I was happy to be back in my old time slot again but I didn't feel challenged enough. The last two months of filling in on the morning show really took my learning to a level it hadn't been before. Listening became my biggest challenge. On a morning show you converse back and forth with a co-host the majority of the time. There are solo morning shows out there, but they are very few and far between. They teach you a lot in school, but one thing they don't harp on is listening, there is no course on how to attentively listen to somebody and this therefore was something that kept me on my toes, and I enjoyed that but I just don't think I was ready for it. My confidence wasn't quite at that level. So, my mind started to race.

I didn't exactly know what would take me there, but I knew I had to try. For the longest time I had a clear vision of wanting to live in beautiful British Columbia. It was almost five thousand kilometers across the country. How could I make this possible? Radio seemed to make the most sense at the time as there were several job posts for the West Coast. I also remembered what my radio friend from Toronto told me: "Go write your story." So that's what I continued to do.

I started applying out west. I lost out on several jobs and then all of a sudden, one clicked. His name was Mark, the program director for Sun FM in Kelowna and 20 other radio stations in the B.C. interior. He offered me a networked mid-day show in Kelowna, B.C., in 2004, which would not just air in Kelowna, but Penticton, Vernon, and online.

I accepted.

My Toronto radio friend also told me that, "If you're good enough and they want you bad enough, the radio station will often front the bill and move you out there." He said, "It's a write off for them, so it's not the biggest deal in the world."

My hard work had paid off. My fiancé at the time, Marilena, and I were moved out west. Incredible. A dream come true.

It was a sideways move career wise, and I knew that. Going from one medium market in Canada to another and going from evenings to taking on mid-days, but the dream of living and working in B.C. was too vivid and I'm so grateful to Mark for fulfilling that dream.

You know how they say the grass isn't always greener on the other side? Well, the grass wasn't greener on the other side of Canada, at least in my opinion, anyway. The Okanagan was often referred to as Canada's sunshine capital. It's what enticed me to want to move out there. Sunshine, the mountains, and the lakes. I was told a few times that it was essentially the Canadian California.

A little piece of advice, and I don't mean this negatively, whenever you hear of a destination or a city/town or country that promotes they have sunshine, i.e. "Canada's Sunshine Capital", don't believe them! Weather will be weather, especially in Canada.

I have often heard another saying. "If you don't like the weather in Canada, just wait ten minutes." So, this idea that the Okanagan is Canada's version of California is false, in my opinion. Mind you, I only lived out there for a year, so maybe I caught a bad year weather wise? What hurt was that the notion of chasing after sunshine and good weather with the lakes and the mountains was a part of the dream for me. That part about the sunshine wasn't fulfilled unfortunately. Well, it was, but not as much as I would have liked it to be. Know what I mean?

Maybe I should have worked in the Cayman Islands. In B.C. my wife and I always felt like we were chasing the sun and whenever lacking sun big time, folks in B.C. would tell you to head to the top of Big White. So, let me get something straight here, you are considered Canada's sunshine capital, but in order to get sun most days in the winter you have to go to Big White and stand at the top of a ski hill? Come on. What is that?

My wife and I weren't the only ones feeling the effects of the lack of natural vitamin D. We went hiking often with another couple, and they told us they had a friend from Edmonton who tried to move out to the Okanagan in the winter and he lasted a week. Sure, he could have given it more of a chance, but I guess he was *really* feeling blue because of it. Thing is, in Edmonton your winters are blistering cold, but you get sunshine and a blue sky more often than not. If I had to guess, he saw seven days of thick, dark clouds with fog when he moved to the Okanagan. Some people like that scene though. He obviously didn't, and we didn't. I remember at one point actually counting the days I didn't see the sun. I think we went thirteen days in a row at one point without it.

Now, all of that being said, I'll give it to them. The province is absolutely breathtaking and stunning with the backdrop that is their mountains. When you do get sunshine, it's the most beautiful part of Canada that I have ever seen.

It was a hot, sunny afternoon on the long, Labour Day weekend of 2006 when I first arrived in B.C., and who else would be picking me up at the airport other than my friend Dan!

Dan was the former afternoon drive guy at KISS 92. This was probably the third time we had crossed paths in the radio business. What you begin to realize is, this business is *small*. Everyone knows everyone, for the most part. So, I never wanted to burn any bridges.

Dan was hosting the morning show at Sun FM at the time with his co-host Susan, and I was going to be the lucky guy on the air after them, hosting 9am-2pm on weekdays. Most of us had voice tracking duties on top of our LIVE shows. Dan had his shades on when he picked me up. It looked exactly like the Okanagan Valley that I had imagined. Lots of sunshine with the mountains and valleys in the background.

Dan and I gave one another a *huge* hug. We hopped in his orange, fancy sports car. Windows were rolled down and some music playing. I was in heaven on day one.

When he dropped me off at my hotel, he told me to let him know if I needed anything and to just call. I had been set up in a hotel for a couple weeks until I found a place in the Okanagan. Marilena, who was still my fiancé back then, hadn't moved with me yet because she had to take care of a few things back home. She planned on moving in October. It was the beginning of September, so my main focus outside of work hours was to find a place to live that she would like.

Happy wife, happy life. Right? Right.

I dropped my bags in my hotel room. *First thing's first, I'm going to spend some time outside exploring beautiful British Columbia.* And boy was it ever beautiful on that sunny afternoon. I walked to the park; it was 10 minutes from where I was staying. The mountains were stunning. I had never seen anything like them before. I had never even been to the West Coast before, believe it or not. This was my first time.

I was 21. I noticed people were roller blading, bike riding, jogging, and walking their dogs. They were enjoying their ice cream while going for a walk by the lake. I couldn't believe this was steps away from where I'd be working and living. This was the dream and it came true with a lot of hard work and determination. I soaked up those few moments and held on to them as long as I could. Staring out at the lake I remembered I had to call my mom and my wife to let them know I had arrived safely.

There was a pay phone in the park. Remember those? It was not too far from the lake. I didn't get my own cell phone until I turned 25. And even then, I shared it with my wife. I had no interest in cell phones back then; can't say the same now.

I put my quarter into the pay phone and took my calling card out of my murse. A murse is a fanny pack, also known as a purse made for a guy. At least that's what some people call them, including me. I punched in my parents' phone number. *Ring, ring* and my parents answered. I was so excited to tell them how much I loved the city of Kelowna already, after only being there for a few hours.

They joined in on my excitement. Next, to call my wife. "Hey Rob, how was the flight?" she asked.

I responded with, "Good," and then I immediately moved to explaining how breathtaking this place was. The mountains, the sunshine, the lake. All of it!

"Ya? That's cool," she replied nonchalantly. I could sense some nervousness in her voice. She was happy for what I was describing to her, but I knew the hesitancy she was portraying was towards not being able to see her family as often. That's why she didn't believe the hype in moving so far away, especially to a place very foreign to her. I have to give her credit though, she was about to follow me almost five thousand kilometers across the country to a region we had no close family and friends in just so she could be by my side as I fulfilled this dream, this vision of mine, to live out in B.C. Luckily her work in Ontario was about to allow her to work online from Kelowna. I was so grateful for that; she was so grateful for that too and here we were about to try and make this all work.

My first day at the radio station was the Tuesday after Labour Day weekend. The studio was, and still is, on Bernard Avenue in Kelowna. The look out through the studio window was spectacular. You could see the mountains and the lake beyond City Park, and just like that I was on the air! Radio moves are typically fast.

Management needs someone in place by a certain day and time. They have deadlines just like everyone else. It took me a few days to learn the ropes and to eventually meet all my co-workers. They were a tight-knit group of radio people, something I certainly admired.

Marilena eventually arrived in B.C. and moved in with me in late October. She approved of the place I found for us to live in. It was a nice, new condo that was about a ten-minute bike ride from the radio station. I say bike ride because we only had one vehicle with us out west, Marilena's car. The vehicle was standard (stick shift) and I had some great difficulty driving standard. I even took a few lessons about a year later. I learned, but I still found it beyond challenging and uncomfortable.

So, bike riding it was, and it's not like it wasn't an enjoyable bike ride. Mountains all around you with fresh air and it was good for the environment. That's certainly something I noticed when moving out there. The air. It seemed a lot cleaner than the big city. We were set. My wife was working from home and I was working at the radio station.

As the year moved on, learning became the norm. As it should be. This was a networked mid-day show that I was hosting. Hadn't done anything like it before. I had to export talk segments to two other markets in the Okanagan Valley even though I was not LIVE in those markets. The exporting made it seem like I was though. There's your little sneak peek of the magic of radio for ya. It was a way for one person to do three jobs on one salary. A salary I was certainly grateful for because it fulfilled my dream and my vision of living in beautiful B.C.

One of my favorite parts of the radio station in Kelowna was the coffee machine. I'm a coffee connoisseur. I absolutely love the taste of all kinds of coffee. Cuban coffee is one of my favorites and I loved the coffee that was available for staff at Standard Radio in Kelowna.

When I met my co-worker Kevin, I immediately took a liking to him, his on-air style, and how he conducted himself on the air and in the hallways. I could tell I was like him, a hard worker, a go getter, and always trying to succeed. It's paid off for him now, as he's currently a morning man on a radio station in Vancouver. I did whatever I could not to emulate Kevin though, even though I was tempted at times. I needed to keep practicing *my* style and delivery. Kevin was, and still is, very good at what he does.

A friend of mine in the radio business named Cory often tried to instill something in my brain back when I was in Toronto and we were both working at CHUM-FM together. I should not be trying to copy the sound and style of other on-air hosts. If there's anyone I always wanted to be like, on the air and off, though, it was Cory. What a great example he set. I interned for him back in the day when I was 16 years old and just starting out. I absolutely loved his style and creativity on air, but most of all I loved his personality on and off the air.

His personality equals the nicest guy on the planet! Someone who would give you the jacket off their back in a heartbeat if it meant helping you out. He thoroughly enjoys helping good people, and when I was interning for him all I wanted to do was help him. It was a good connection we had and we worked well together.

There came a point though where, for the greater good, Cory told me not to listen to him on the air for a month because he wanted me to find my own greatness as a personality. I had been emulating him and sounded a whole lot like him too. To top it off we were both on the air at the same radio station, just in different time slots.

You don't want two of the same people.

What can I say? I was nineteen at the time and I hadn't quite figured out who I was on the air just yet, so I wanted to be like Cory. Another radio friend of mine, Frank, even recalled hearing me on the air at CHUM-FM after a concert in Toronto and he had asked someone who he was in the car with at the time if that was Cory he had just heard? The resemblance certainly was uncanny and Cory and I still to this day sound similar, but I've learned to be my own person.

It's all about being your own unique you while trying to figure out what you want to be remembered for. That's what my former boss Julie taught me. She said to me, "Rob, what are the 5 things you want to be remembered for?" when giving me an aircheck one day. For me, it's to be genuine, creative, kind, a little funny, not a lot but a little, and having passion. That method that Julie brought to my attention really helped me in discovering who I am on the air and off. By the way, Cory and I have been good friends for 20 years now. He is who you hear on the air. Very authentic. He also has such a big heart and I'm so grateful we met and have stayed connected all these years. Knowing him certainly has made me a better person.

For some, moving to Kelowna means you never turn back. That's how much certain people fall in love with it. The great hiking trails, the toys that come out in the summer time—boats, motorcycles, RVs, and more—but for Marilena and I, we were really starting to miss family and began to feel how far we actually were from home. We tried to embrace what was right in front of us though, the hiking trails, the beaches, going to Kelowna Rockets hockey games, and enjoying the great outdoors.

It was all fantastic, but at the end of the day it was missing something. It didn't feel like home. And that's ok. I was there for the experience first and foremost. Home is where the heart is. Home to us is Vaughan, Ontario. We were 2,500 miles away from it in the beautiful Okanagan Valley, which I really loved, but as I've stated before, the weather didn't live up to the expectations I had back then. B.C. was where I really started to develop seasonal affective disorder.

In the winter in Ontario we would get some grey days, but nowhere near the amount that B.C. gets, or at least got when I lived there for a year. The grey in B.C. next to Ontario is also different, here it's either just a thin or dark grey color. In B.C.'s Okanagan Valley it is very foggy and the grey clouds tend to swoop in on top of the lake, almost looking like they're touching the water. When you throw in the fact that the Okanagan is a valley with no real high-rise buildings that I was used to living around, I ultimately got the fish bowl and socked in effect.

I recall flying back home once and when the plane took off, I looked down to see that we were essentially flying out of some kind of bubble. The thick, dark, storm-like clouds would hover over the mountain tops and the next thing you knew, a few moments would pass and we were high enough that the sky turned blue and there was bright sunshine. Aside from the weather uncertainty and missing family, I loved my job. My co-workers were great and I felt challenged in my daily work routine.

About nine months into the job in Kelowna my boss could tell Marilena and I were homesick. I always knew this didn't have to be forever. The dream was to live in B.C. There was no length of time we had to stay.

I began to send out airchecks again. I had seen an opening for full-time evenings at MIX 99.9 in Toronto, so I sent my audition package in. Little did I know at the time that program directors within the same work company correspond frequently. They have work meetings, speak on the phone, and email.

So, one day my boss in Kelowna came up to me in the office. He seemed quite frustrated, rightfully so, that I had sent an audition tape out to the MIX in Toronto without giving him the heads up first. Turns out the program director in Toronto, Karen, notified my current boss that I sent something in for evenings. I never did end up getting the job and I apologized to my boss.

I never again sent out an audition package to a radio station within the same company I was currently working for without notifying my boss first. Eventually another opportunity rolled around within the same company I was currently working for, Standard Radio. Evenings at MIX 96 Montreal. I had dreamed of working for this station! I had always been fascinated with it. I loved the music they played. It was similar to what I was playing in Kelowna, which was a variety of pop, current hits, and music from the 80's and 90's too. Certainly, a fantastic variety.

What was also intriguing was that this stop could potentially get my wife and I one step closer to getting back home one day and put another major market on my resume. Or maybe you fall in love with Montreal so much that you end up calling it home? That did not happen actually. Having said that, I do always call it my second home. And speaking of home, we would be a lot closer to Toronto if I landed this gig in Montreal.

It was either a five and a half hour drive or an hour plane ride away from the suburbs of the Greater Toronto Area. I also always wanted to work in Montreal. It certainly was another dream of mine, a vision that I had growing up. I have a ton of family there and it's almost like you could call it the central meeting grounds for my family when we have huge gatherings for certain Jewish holidays.

I'm Jewish and Marilena is Italian. Our families have a lot of similarities and get along really well.

I also enjoy the food in Montreal and the nightlife is top notch. In Toronto and surrounding areas we live to work. In Montreal they work to live. Nothing wrong with either, but I was about to experience the latter.

When I was a kid, I used to tell my parents to tell our close family and friends that I was born in Montreal and not Toronto; that's how much I loved the city. Bob was the gentleman's name who was about to fulfill a massive dream of mine. He was the program director for MIX 96 Montreal and liked my sound on the air when he was listening to me online from Kelowna. Turns out he liked it so much that he was willing to move my wife and I thousands of miles across the country, this time to La Belle Province so I could host his evening show on the MIX and write the weekly top 30 countdown for his morning team.

I made sure I did things right this time. Since MIX 96 Montreal and Sun FM were under the same company umbrella, I told my boss in Kelowna, Mark, that I was going to send an audition tape prior to sending it in.

He was alright with it and ended up in conversation with Bob about me frequently at the time. I'd be in the office in Kelowna and Mark would say, "Hey Rob, they were listening to you again today in Montreal."

My heart stopped at that moment. I felt so thankful. I've always been someone that never believed in their own hype. If someone were to listen to me on the air, I'd be eternally grateful, and I can't tell you how good it feels when management at a radio station you've always wanted to work for begins to listen to you too. Wow, cloud nine. Was this for real? I think I had to pinch myself. I always knew that, because I didn't speak much French, the only way I was going to be able to work in Montreal was if I were to be hired by one of the two radio clusters that had English-speaking stations in the city, and Bob was about to make that happen.

As I've said before, radio moves usually happen fast, and this one was no different. Our movers this time around were the official movers of the professional football team that's based in Montreal. My boss tried to ensure we had the smoothest move possible, so he went with one of the best, and Marilena and I were impressed with the results.

The movers packed up our condo on a Saturday, they loaded everything up on Sunday, we flew out on Monday, and my first day on the air in Montreal was Tuesday. *Whirlwind!* But I wouldn't have had it any other way. Before we flew out, I made sure to embrace those last few moments in B.C. We had lived there for just over a year. It wasn't everything I had hoped for and more, but I was certainly proud to have lived out my dream there. It was a friend of mine by the name of Rhonda who dropped us off at the airport in Kelowna. I worked with her at the radio station in the Okanagan and she was nice enough to allow us to stay the night so we didn't have to go to a hotel due to our entire condo already being packed up.

Marilena and I frequently went hiking with her. B.C. is certainly known for their incredible hiking trails. We thanked Rhonda for her hospitality and off we went.

We landed in Toronto on Monday night and had dinner with some of our family and friends at a restaurant inside the airport in Toronto. Why the airport you might ask? I had a connecting flight to Montreal that would leave later that night while my wife would stay back in Toronto to work until I got us settled in Montreal. It was so nice seeing my family and friends again. I tried to soak up every minute of what was going on. The restaurant was great but the company was better. I said my goodbyes and the next thing

Beyond The Mic

you know the following adventure was waiting. I was about to board another plane, this time destined for the great city of Montreal.

When I landed in Montreal, Mark picked me up at the airport. He was the afternoon drive show host and music director at the time for the radio station I was hired at, and it turned out we had a lot in common. A genuine passion for radio for the most part and lots of love for the Montreal Canadiens, the city's hockey team. Before I got to the hotel we stopped at a local bar where you could say we had some "Welcome to Montreal shots." It was a lot of fun.

I arrived at the hotel later that night and that's when it began to sink in. I was alone. I knew my wife would eventually join me, but I couldn't help shedding a few tears and I knew it wasn't because of the alcohol. This happened to me often actually, mostly every time I had moved. I don't mind moving, but you get emotional; at least I do anyway. I cried, unpacked my stuff and eventually went to sleep.

I had six weeks to find a place, so the hotel was home for the next little while. It was a hotel and an apartment all in one. I had a stove so I could cook and a small dining area too. I'm a horrible cook though, so it was mostly readymade meals that I'd get at the grocery store or Montreal restaurant food. My uncle who lived in a Montreal suburb would give me the Montreal food tour and treat me to some dinners here and there. The food in Montreal is incredible. There was this specific greasy spoon spot across the street from the hotel that was a breakfast place. Not sure it still exists. I hope so! I also don't see why not.

I took my father there when he came to visit and he approved too. We both had the bacon and eggs special, which came with "miniature" hash browns and a side of pancakes. The portions were quite generous there. The hash browns filled at least half our plate and we were given about seven bacon strips each. We made sure to come hungry though, so all was devoured in one sitting, right to the last crumb.

I had trouble finding a place for my wife and I to live. That's why my dad came to visit. He wanted to help me during the day before I'd go into work at night. He spoke French, and I did not, so it helped when trying to retrieve more information about certain apartments that were available.

Time went on and still no such luck with the apartment search. We wanted to make sure we had indoor parking for Marilena's car because it snowed a lot more in Montreal than it did in Kelowna in the winter time. A lot of times in Montreal when you rent, there is no indoor parking option available to you, which is probably cheaper for the landlord. We were not a fan of street parking in Montreal though. Have you seen the winters there?

As a kid I'd play pick-up hockey with my dad on outdoor rinks there. When walking back to our car after the game, I used to see massive squares of white snow up against the curb. Turns out that wasn't just snow I was staring at. Those were vehicles boxed in by snow that covered practically your entire vehicle. Imagine it stays like that overnight? There ain't no way you're getting into your vehicle the next morning for how frozen shut it would be, that's for sure. I thanked my dad for the visit to Montreal, and before he went back to Toronto I asked if he wouldn't mind apartment shopping online for me while I also looked during the day. We didn't want to give up.

At last, we found it! My wife and I were going to live on De Maisonneuve Avenue West in Westmount, a suberb of Montreal, a real nice one at that. It was expensive, but hey, you get what you pay for, and I wasn't about to go taking chances on living conditions, because it wouldn't just affect my life, but Marilena's too. I can't thank our family friend Nives enough for driving me around from apartment to apartment trying to find the right one. She was certainly an integral part of the apartment search having combed through the Montreal Gazette as well as looking online. I'm so grateful. Nives lives in Montreal West and I became really close friends with her and her husband Mauro, their three sons, and family friend Giorgio.

I often felt like I was re-living my childhood by playing pick-up hockey with some of the boys on Saturday afternoons or Sunday evenings on outdoor rinks. It was so much fun and great exercise too. We never played on Saturday nights though. Saturday nights were reserved for keeping warm indoors with a nice spread of Lester's smoked meat, rye bread, and fries for dinner followed by some hot chocolate. Not immediately after, but just in time for puck drop between our Montreal Canadiens and whomever the opponent would have been.

I loved being surrounded by Montreal Canadiens fans. I spent most of my life surrounded by Toronto hockey fans, so this was a welcomed change. The apartment we'd be living in was steps away from Vendome metro station, not to be confused by the supermarket Metro. The metro is Montreal's transit system. I was always intrigued with how fast the trains would go. I'd think to myself, *Toronto has "Ride The Rocket" for their subway slogan, but have they ever experienced Montreal's?*

It was incredible. You might need Gravol after a ride on Montreal's metro system for how nauseous you could get. It was that fast. Maybe that's going too far, but I think you know what I mean. If you don't, the next time you go to Just For Laughs in Montreal or for a steak dinner in the old port, try taking the metro. It's also easier than driving there. Potholes are scattered on several roads and streets in Montreal and most of the drivers don't believe in signaling when changing lanes. The combination of the two drives me nuts!

On a more positive note, the location of the new apartment couldn't have been better. It was just a few short metro stops away from work for me. Everything is very centralized in Montreal. Unless you're talking about the South Shore or the West Island, you're mostly five to ten minutes away from everything. Location didn't really matter too much for my wife though, she would be working online again, like she did in Kelowna, this time with more frequent business trips to Toronto.

Her boss was happier with her being closer to Toronto and I can't thank him enough for finding a way to keep Marilena working remotely. It really meant a lot to me. While she worked from home she needed a space to call her own. So, part of our living room ended up turning into Marilena's office. The apartment was spacious, so it worked.

In terms of the apartment building itself, it included indoor parking and that wasn't the only thing that was included indoors. A swimming pool was on the top floor of the building. Glass windows enclosed it with an incredible, breathtaking view of the entire city of Montreal and surrounding areas. Before my injury, I used to swim a lot of lengths there. It would help with weight loss and I certainly found it helped manage my mental health too. What was super convenient was the fact that grocery stores were very close to the apartment, we also had local parks and soccer fields nearby, plus we had a spare bedroom for friends and family that wanted to visit.

We had a lot of visitors, which solidified our popularity back home. That, or everyone just needed a free place to stay when visiting one of the best cities in North America. Free loaders! I kid, I kid. We were happy whenever friends and family wanted to visit. Thankful is more like it.

The time had come. Our items and furniture had arrived from the West Coast after being in storage. I could tell our furniture had been carefully handled too. Nothing was broken and all that there was left to do was unpack, welcome Marilena when she arrived later that month, and eventually decorate.

When Marilena moved in, she arrived to a typical, cold, snowy Montreal winter. I'm not the biggest fan of winter—you might not be either—but I can handle it in doses, and like most Canadians I just wish the season itself was a lot shorter. Once January 1st arrives, it's like bring me spring weather already. Please? I'd have to move to California for that to happen, but I try to keep this quote handy when needed, "Happiness is not a place—it is a direction." And the direction to go in at the time was being the best on-air personality and writer I could be for **MIX 96** while getting accustomed to and enjoying life with my wife in a new city and a new province.

The average annual snowfall in Montreal was anywhere between 150-300cm with blistering cold temperatures too. What made it so cold was the nasty wind chill. When it was really bad, you'd walk outside and, if your skin wasn't covered up, you'd have frostbite within a few minutes. What was the solution for this? Sporting my oven-like **MIX 96** winter jacket. I tell ya, there's something about receiving radio station swag that always makes things better. Perhaps it makes you feel more a part of the team. It also may have saved my life from that nasty wind chill!

I took an enormous amount of pride in being a part of the great team at the MIX in Montreal. There, I went by the name RJ Daniels on the air. The name Rob had been taken before I got there, so I totally understood that I had to go with a different stage name. My bosses were the ones who gave me the new name. They liked how the initials sounded together, and so did I. Everyone at the MIX was dedicated to delivering the best radio product possible while still trying to have fun, and we had a lot of fun. I hosted club nights with the radio station a couple of weekends a month.

We always had a routine when I worked Montreal club nights. Work, party, do some more work, and end up going out for poutine, smoked meat, or both in the middle of the night after the club gig wrapped up. Montreal poutine is the best. I can't eat that kind of food late at night anymore though. Funny how your stomach ages with you. What I used to be able to stomach at all times of the day makes me feel incredibly sick nowadays. I enjoyed my twenties while they lasted.

The job was incredible, it was everything I had ever dreamed of and more. If I could have changed one thing, I'd say it would have been to work daytime hours Monday to Friday instead of hosting the evening show. This way I could have spent more time with Marilena in the evenings and on the weekends, but you know what they say, beggars can't be choosers and absence makes the heart grow fonder.

What was intriguing in all this was I began to get recognized for my work in Montreal outside of the studio. Listeners would come up to me at radio station events, introduce themselves and tell me how certain talk segments of mine really resonated with them and their families. That felt good. You don't necessarily get that all the time in say Toronto, New York City, or Los Angeles. In those cities you *really* have to find a way to stick out amongst a huge pack of other incredibly talented radio broadcasters, and of course, great music, in order to cut through and really get noticed. Life was good though and I was grateful.

One day on a cold winter morning, the entire staff at work was called in for a meeting. My gut was telling me change was on the horizon. It turned out we were re-branding from MIX 96 to Virgin Radio. Same format, just a fresh coat of paint. However, my duties were about to change. I was no longer the main event beyond the music in the evening time slot. That role would end up being given to a certain individual via syndication out of Los Angeles.

I was informed I'd be producing his show and then hosting two hours on my own on-air Monday through Thursday from 10pm-midnight. I'd still keep my Sunday afternoon four hour, on-air time slot and my writing duties for the morning show would not change. The only constant was change when it came to the radio business, something I always knew but only started to really grasp when it affected me, and this was the first time. So, I decided to go for a walk that morning and eventually returned to accept my new duties. I've always tried my best to make the most of every situation.

I did what I could to make the most of the curve ball I had been thrown and the situation I was in. I was still a full-time employee on a radio station in the beautiful city of Montreal. We enjoyed the city's nightlife, the food, and the festivals. And work was still fun. Someone once told me, "Whenever radio is no longer fun, that's when you should stop doing it." Great quote. With that being said, my boss knew I didn't move just over 4,000 kilometers across Canada from Kelowna, B.C. to Montreal, Quebec for the job I was currently undertaking, so he made it clear to me that he understood if I decided to look for something else. Something more me. That something else was KiSS 92.5 in Toronto. Yup, I was about to go full circle.

I had to do a double take when I saw the job post for KiSS 92.5. Was this for real? It was! The station I had dreamed of being an on-air personality for when I was 16 years old was returning with its top 40 format in Toronto. JACK-FM, which originally took over for KISS in 2003, was about to flip formats again. New pop artists were about to be introduced to the world and eventually blow up in fame in front of our very own eyes. It took me a while to convince the program director at KiSS that I should be on the air there.

With not having a full time show in Montreal that aired weekdays and working on a slightly different format than KiSS, I often sent her emails asking if she wouldn't mind listening to me when I was filling in during the day. That way I could try and impress her. To me, every day is an audition. It doesn't matter who is listening, I always try and put out a solid product on the air. I couldn't wait to hear what KiSS sounded like again, and of course everything in me wanted to be a part of the team that helped launch the new station.

There was one full time, on-air opening left at this incredible radio station in Toronto that I had dreamed of being a part of on the air ever since I was 16 years old. I was 25 at the time, and, with all the passion and perseverance I put into the application process, I was so grateful to find out that I landed the job! My heart was beating incredibly fast when I took the phone call from the KiSS 92.5 Toronto program director in my Montreal apartment. She told me something along the lines of: "Even though you don't have a lot of on-air time at the moment, you have some great references who backed up your talent." Ultimately, that's how she came to the decision of hiring me. That moment in time froze for a couple of seconds and tears rolled down my cheeks as the news began to sink in.

We were going home.

Back to the city where it all started for my wife and I. Another dream about to come true. My wife had been anticipating this phone call even more than me. Home is where the heart is and that couldn't be more true for her. Family is everything to her. It is to me too, but there's just something different about the Italian heritage. Their sense of closeness. Sometimes living more than a four kilometer drive from immediate family is considered too far for parents if you've grown up in an Italian family. All good. They are next level family appreciators.

As much as that can be conflicting to someone chasing their dreams, leaving your family for a bit and all, the immense level of closeness with family is ultimately something very special too, and it should never be taken for granted. Marilena was ecstatic, her grin was glowing and those dimples that would form in her cheeks from time to time began to make an appearance again. Her excitement was infectious.

It was a Friday night and Marilena and I were about to go to a restaurant on Crescent Street to celebrate the good news. First, we wanted to tell our family and friends. Everyone was really happy for us, especially one of Marilena's friends. Her name was Jennifer. She had long, black hair and had known Marilena ever since they were kids. About a couple weeks into moving to Kelowna, B.C. Jennifer would jokingly tell me, "Rob, I'm allowing you to have five more months with her and then you have to bring her home!" Shows you how really close of friends they were and that was also her way of poking fun at the situation with me. From what I recall, I always used to just laugh it off. I didn't really know what to say in response.

You see, to me, I could live anywhere. Granted, I loved knowing when I'd be returning home for visits so I'd have something to look forward to, but I don't need to live in just one city all the time. Guess that's part of the reason why the radio industry and I have gotten along so well over the years, minus the business decisions made that weren't in my favor of course. But the moving around part I enjoyed because I got to experience life in different facets. If you want a really successful, long standing career in radio there's a chance you could be seeing most of the country you're living in. It's not always the case, but sometimes. This too, could be an industry for you if you don't mind uncertainty and you love to travel.

Most jobs in this day in age are uncertain anyway, but radio has always been known for uncertainty a little more than usual. I guess the word I'm looking for is instability, but I also do believe if you're good enough at what you do and you've cast a wide enough net you will find work. And work is what I found at Toronto's KiSS 92.5.

I was hired as a full-time swing announcer. I would be on the air Thursdays and Fridays 9am-2pm and Saturdays and Sundays from 4pm-10pm. The entire weekend was shot, but hey, when you love what you do for a living it's a small sacrifice to make. You might be wondering, *How do you receive a full-time salary on just a four-day work week?*

The answer to that question is, not every week was a four-day work week. At times, I'd be required to fill in for others on the air which would sometimes give me a seven- or eight-day work week without a day off in between. It all balanced out in the end.

Cue up "Home" by Daughtry. We were headed for Toronto.

August 12th, 2009 was my last day at the office and on the air in Montreal. I loved living in that city. I loved working in that city. However, I knew my waistline would be better off by not living in that city. The food was too good. Nothing happens by chance though. There were obviously other reasons for leaving too. Nonetheless, I was going to miss it there. I considered it my second home. Don't cry because it's over, smile because it happened. That was the best way to look at it.

Mar left for Toronto first while I continued to live in our Montreal apartment until it was signed off on. The weekend before I officially left Montreal, I decided to take a mini road trip with my dad and my brother before I kicked off the new journey at KiSS in Toronto. I took the train to Kingston, Ontario, met up with my dad and my brother, who also took the train but from Toronto to Kingston. We met halfway and then proceeded to rent a car and leave for Cooperstown, N.Y. We always wanted to see the baseball hall of fame and we thought this was the perfect time to go. It was fantastic. Just think Disney World for a huge baseball fan. That was Cooperstown. It turned out to be a great visit.

Labour Day weekend 2009 rolled around, and the nerves were at an all-time high. I was happy to be home but super nervous for my first day at KiSS, which was in just a few short days. I didn't know what to expect. I had never been in that kind of a situation before. What do I mean by that exactly? To be a part of a launch team. You see, the first era of KISS 92 in Toronto ended with a format flip to JACK-FM in 2003. JACK-FM lasted until 2009 on the air in Toronto, and that's when the second era of KiSS 92.5 began. The changeover occurred in the summer of 2009 to be a little more specific. So we were a brand new radio station, with brand-new staff, essentially saying "Let's get this thing off the ground and run with it!" We did just that.

The ice was officially broken at the staff photo shoot between my co-workers and I, and those co-workers are some of my best friends in the business today. Hand chosen and crafted by one of the most respected Canadian radio programmers in the country. That's also Toronto for you of course. You don't get the opportunity to work on the air in Toronto unless you're incredibly gifted at your craft. It also didn't matter how long you stayed in the city for either. You were respected either way, some more than others.

Toronto is a tough market to spend your entire career in due to all the change. You're either a part of the change or you're not. An old friend in Montreal, who sadly passed away a few years ago, told me, "Rob, you're only as good as your program director thinks you are," and I think that stands true. Not only in the radio industry but for any line of work really. Maybe that's why many folks flock at the opportunity to become their own boss, easier to avoid the pressure that way. I'm not sure. What I was sure of, was that my time at KiSS from 2009-2011 wasn't the amazing experience I had hoped it would be.

I lived out the dream of being on the air at KiSS, that's for sure, but I didn't turn out to be as successful as I wanted to be. That may have been my fault; I'm not sure. I made a few mistakes, but I also think I made up for those mistakes. Perhaps I made too many mistakes for a Toronto radio station on-air performer? In reality there were multiple factors.

This was a time in my life where I was comparing myself to others frequently, and at times became jealous of the success others were having around me while I felt like I wasn't climbing the ladder. I was verbal about my concerns in some one-on-one staff meetings, but ultimately I think voicing those types of concerns put me on the negativity list—if there is one of those. I was being a Negative Nancy. It's been 10 years since then though, I know I've changed for the better, and I no longer get jealous. Sometimes our mindsets need a reset, and that's what happened with me. I reset my mindset to practice gratitude for what I do have, rather than practicing a piss poor attitude for what I don't have or may think I deserve. Perhaps I lacked some confidence back then and it was showing? You never really know if you're getting the full truth when being let go.

I do know one thing. I did comprehend, upon my departure, that I didn't have a big enough brand—a big enough social media following—and that's one of the reasons I was shown the door. Bosses and management are always scouring the internet for your activity on social media, don't be blind to it. So, make sure you're proud of your social media activity, or at least be careful how you conduct yourself on it. Don't be afraid to be you, but just be careful is all I'm saying.

Did you know that there still hasn't been one single proven stat that shows a direct correlation of your social media following equaling how great or not great your ratings are? I don't get it. Part of me feels like once social media was embraced by the radio industry, it kind of ruined the radio industry too. Whether it's checking how many likes you have, how many followers, how you portray yourself with filters, it can all be very damaging to one's mental health. Did the people who came up with it realize this? Maybe, but it's a money maker, and there are far worse money makers for your mental and physical health out there.

The other issue was I was told by one of my managers that she didn't get who Robbie D was. She didn't fully understand who I actually was on the air. I think more than anything, management at KiSS specifically want your personality to shine, but they also want you to develop into a character for your show too. Not every radio station wants that, but KiSS did.

A perfect example at this would be their current morning show. You can tell that all the on-air members of the morning show portray their own character, and they stick with it throughout their tenure. Perhaps they were right, perhaps I was lacking the character part. So now what? The dream had been fulfilled but it kind of felt shattered at the same time. My ego took a big hit too whenever change was not on my side in the workforce, and I've never had a big ego to begin with. I really started to struggle with my confidence. *Who am I? Was this my fault? Can I still make a living at this?* The anxiety seemed worse than it had been over the last couple of years. Then there were days where it was like, *You got this Rob. You'll land on your feet.*

In the end, I remained hopeful and continued to pound the pavement to try and find out what was next.

I left on good terms with management at KiSS. That opened the door for a new opportunity just down the road in Kitchener at KiSS 92.5's sister station CHYM 96.7. A heritage adult contemporary radio station. I could relate to it big time and I felt more laid back than I did at KiSS. There wasn't competition coming at you from all angles. I mean, you never want to be lackadaisical with your work, so I continued to work hard. I hosted Saturdays 7am-1pm and weekday fill-in when needed.

The stint was very short lived though. A brand new opportunity similar to the one I had recently had at KiSS was offered to me at 99.9 Virgin Radio in Toronto. It was part-time weekends and fill-in, but I still jumped all over it knowing it was permanent part-time. Whereas, at CHYM, it was one day a week plus fill-in on a temporary basis with the chance of going permanent. This wasn't my last stop in Kitchener/Waterloo though. I'd be back shortly. For now, it was off to 2 St. Clair Avenue West in Toronto.

Some of the best program directors and assistant program directors in the radio industry are the ones that never stop being coaches. I understand having to adhere to the manager side of it, but never lose sight of helping make your on-air staff the best possible staff there is. Look at me trying to tell program directors how to do their jobs! Maybe it's because I've always been a student of the game and that's why I've always appreciated receiving feedback from my bosses. When it comes to trying to better my craft, I'm usually up for the challenge.

My assistant program director at Virgin Radio Toronto would have been put under that umbrella of an assistant program director that was a teacher, and boy did he teach me a lot when I was there.

Virgin Radio Toronto was where I did a ton of learning in my career, there and at my first and second stop in Kitchener/Waterloo at the BEAT. I started to really feel comfortable at 2 St. Clair

Avenue West, but not for long because I noticed a merger was about to take place. I had been at Virgin Radio Toronto for about a year and a half. The next thing I knew another company had purchased us. When that happens it usually means change. It's rare that it doesn't, and this time was no different. Change was on the horizon, and I wasn't a part of that change unfortunately. I found myself out of an on-air job, again. Back to square one.

At this point I was well into a part-time teaching opportunity, a couple of them actually, at two separate community colleges in Ontario. I was teaching Announcing Skills Level Three and Intro to Radio Sales. I absolutely loved it. Part of me has always been intrigued by being an instructor and helping out the next generation of broadcasters. The other part of me still wanted to be on the air. This was another full circle moment too, because one of the colleges I was teaching at was the one I graduated from. It was very cool to step back into one of the same classrooms, this time as a professor.

The dream at that moment was to pick up some kind of weekdays afternoon drive show, on the air full time while teaching on the side. The stars didn't align that way, but it was all good, because I found myself in a full-time roll on the air in Kitchener/Waterloo again, my second go at 91.5 the beat, which got underway in August of 2014. I was also hired as the music assistant for the beat and brother station DAVE ROCKS. It was great to learn more about the day-to-day duties of a music department. It was more to put on a resume too.

Sometimes you can't have everything turn out exactly the way you want it to in life, you might already know that. The reason teaching didn't work out was because one of the courses I was teaching got discontinued and the others were taken over by my former teacher, who has been around a lot longer than I have in radio and was ready to get back into teaching again. I knew him fairly well, so I couldn't get upset. I mean, he taught me when I was in radio school.

You never really can get upset at business decisions in this industry. It's too small, almost everyone knows everyone, and almost everyone wants another person's job. It's kind of like the teaching world in elementary school and high school. So many talented people, so few jobs. So, what was happening was certainly understandable, and I'm grateful to have fulfilled the dream of teaching at the community college level. Hopefully I can do it again sometime.

For the next three and a half years I was on cloud nine. My show on the beat in Kitchener/Waterloo aired weekdays 9am-2pm and I'd help out in the music department when I got off the air. I hosted remote broadcasts and eventually landed my first-ever weekly live-to-air gig!

Working the live-to-air gig was incredibly cool. Along with listeners partying to hit music and being in attendance to try and unwind after a long week, I was the guy people came to see and counted on for a good time every Friday night. I'm human too, and sometimes had bad nights at the club, but, like any job, you find a way to put your game face on and push through. I found an extra coffee in my day and sometimes an energy drink would help with that.

Marilena constantly reminded me how bad energy drinks were for me though. I appreciated the heads up and I believed her too. I just wasn't ready to put them down anytime soon because I was enjoying making good money and I needed that extra little something that would prevent my eyes from shutting in the wee hours of the morning. My Fridays for a year were: Wake up at 6am and go to bed the next morning at 4. That's twenty-two hours straight of no shut eye.

I hosted middays Fridays 9am-2pm, which was really like a 7:45am -3:30pm day at the office if you include show prep and helping in the music department. Then I'd have a break and work the club late at night. I'm a terrible napper, so most times I had trouble sleeping in between the two gigs, which made days and the hours feel longer. I couldn't be phased though. The sacrifice was worth it. I was living the dream. Every time that mic button went ON, I'd say something to try and make the audience feel like they chose the best place on the planet to party at on a Friday night—with my co-workers and I.

The team usually consisted of our live-to-air producer at the club, the DJ, the producer back at the radio station, and yours truly, the on-air personality. Some nights seemed like the best, others were slow in attendance, but that didn't stop us from trying to get people in the building to buy drinks and get on the dance floor. The tough part was the competition. Some competition is healthy, but there was a little too much for our liking.

Whether it was a brutally cold winter night that nobody wanted to go out on, a festival of sorts in town, construction, or another party down the street in Waterloo in the University district, it always seemed like there was something that was trying to stop us from winning. We really did have some amazing nights at the club from a business stand point, and rocking the mic there on a regular basis really was a dream come true for me. But, once those twelve months went by, business started to go downhill big time.

We had some devastatingly low numbers in attendance in the summer, embarrassing at times. It's a university town and a lot of university students don't live in the Waterloo Region in the summer, so our target audience was barely anywhere to be seen. Plus, the club wasn't really located in the most reputable part of town. That last part always seemed to be up for debate though.

The business troubles eventually lead to my exit and I was shown the door after one full year of live-to-airs on Friday nights. Not a bad run. It was a business decision and that's why it's important to never get too high or too low when in the workforce, same is to be said for life in general. I'll tell you this, anytime I've left a job, whether it was my decision or not, especially a great job that I enjoyed and felt like I was good at, I've tried to leave on good terms, and this was no different.

My departure from the beat occurred about a year and a half after my live-to-air hosting duties ended. Not before taking on some incredible work opportunities though. I was filling in on afternoon drive while management had been searching for their next permanent drive host. The previous host had left to take another opportunity. This meant an opening and you can bet I was doing everything in my power to try and win that position. I made sure management knew I was interested, and I tried not to be a pest about it either. I just made sure to try and show up every day in hopes to make every show better than the one previous. Every day was an audition.

It took longer than normal for a decision to be made. I knew I couldn't let it get the best of me though, especially in a situation like this. What helped keep the anxiety at bay for me was the fact that I knew I'd be ok with returning to the midday show should someone else be hired for drive. I really wanted the afternoon drive show, mostly from a lifestyle perspective, and because it was a new challenge, but I also knew I'd be perfectly ok with returning to what I had been doing. It's a mindset I try to practice frequently. We all try to set goals for ourselves, but I also think we have to be grateful for what we do have, and not always focus on what we don't have or are itching to get.

In this case, patience was a virtue. I had put my head down and let the work do the talking for three months of summer afternoon drive fill in and I was awarded the job. I can't even begin to tell you how happy I was to hear that news. The afternoon drive gig was everything I had hoped for and more. Along with the new on-air role came a new title in the music department. I had been promoted to Assistant Music Director. I felt challenged by both jobs, learning from record reps in the music department weekly while still trying to master my on-air craft in the studio. I was incredibly grateful for both roles. Receiving my shiny, new business cards sweetened the deal even more. Everything had come together nicely in terms of work/life balance. It certainly was a nice feeling.

The only thing I wish I could have had more of, was time. I really thought I could get at least ten years in that position, but the company decided to make restructuring moves at some of their radio properties across Canada in March of 2018, which, as a result, saw my position get completely eliminated from the company.

Get knocked down nine times, stand up ten? That's me. The company that owns 91.5 the beat opened their arms and invited me back in three months later, this time for a morning show role at another one of their radio properties about an hour west of Toronto. I was stoked! I was about to become a morning man.

Beyond The Mic

Mornings didn't last for very long though. I was in and out the door in about two and a half months. I know the title of this book is "Beyond the Mic," but the most I can say here without getting into trouble is that it's sometimes very difficult to have two radio personalities thrown together who had never worked with one another previously and then expecting greatness when they perform together on-air. It either works out well and you have the birth of a really successful morning show, or things don't work out between the two of you. It didn't work out.

Luckily it didn't take very long to land a new gig and get back on the air! I had picked up some weekend and swing on-air work at Virgin Radio in Kitchener/Waterloo. A few months into that position, I was then offered a three-month contract to work the afternoon drive show at 105.9 The Region in York Region. I was working both gigs, keeping busy, and trying to stay positive and remain hopeful. When my contract ended at the Region, I was still working at Virgin Radio Kitchener but not as much as I wanted to.

Then, a couple months later a more permanent part-time position opened up on the air within the same company as Virgin Radio, just down the road in Hamilton. I was hired as 102.9 K-Lite's weekend/swing announcer in Hamilton, ON. I was reporting to work at the studio for a little over three months, and then that's when the world totally flipped upside down.

I'll never forget receiving the word that beginning immediately all announcers except two people from the morning show would have to keep their distance from one another, would have to broadcast their shows from home to try and help stop the spread of Covid-19. So that's what we did. The only constant is change. There were some trials and tribulations. If I had to grade my performance from home, I'd give myself a B. I just found the studio to have more tools for announcers to succeed in and it was less distracting.

If you have your own studio at home things might be different, but I don't and I often found it challenging sound wise to find out where the best possible place in the house was to work. One day my boss said it was the basement. The basement had the best sound quality of the rooms I'd been in according to him. So, my wife moved upstairs to the main floor to work and I worked in the basement. The juggling act for most families due to Covid was beginning to form. We made it work though. When December 2020 rolled around that's when I received news that I was going to be let go from K-Lite.

According to my bosses, being shown the door had nothing to do with my performance. They also told me that "radio is changing at a rapid pace. It's not a good time for radio," and that I had the rest of my December fill in on-air work to complete along with roughly four weekends left to go on air, which three of those weekends would be Saturday work, and not Sunday work. I was slowly sliding out of the on-air schedule. Chin up, it could always be worse.

It's always special when you get to be on the air in your hometown. That's where I'm at now. How did I land my current role of weekends/weekday fill-in when needed at Z103.5 Toronto? Like most gigs in my past. I sent some audio and included references too. I've been in touch with management along with past and present employees of Z103.5 for a very long while, probably since 2006 with a couple of them actually. That may have helped too. You see, the timing/situation was just never right over the years, until now that is. So, how about I slap those headphones on again and give this thing another go. What do you say? Will you join me on the other end? I sure hope so.

Will radio ever die? You hear about the possibility of it frequently. Competition coming at it from all angles. Whether it's video or audio online, podcasts, social media, you name it, there is a lot trying to get a potential listener's attention. That being said, do you remember when satellite radio came out and you heard the buzz that radio then was officially going to die? Thankfully it didn't and I'm so happy it didn't. Hopefully it's not different this time around. Part of me feels that people still enjoy and crave that human one on one connection that's so easy to retrieve with the simple push of a button. As long as radio is around, my hope is to be a part of it in some form or another.

6

MOM & DAD

To have supportive parents is a blessing. I'm so incredibly thankful to be able to call two of the most wonderful human beings I know Mom and Dad.

Whether it was helping me with homework when I was a kid, driving me to my baseball games, doing my laundry, or providing food and shelter, Mom and Dad have always been, and continue to be, supportive. Over the years that support has changed, which is only normal. No longer is Dad quizzing me on math equations on a Sunday morning in hopes for me to succeed on a test at school the next day. Instead, he's playing his guitar and singing songs to my young daughter while I leave the house to catch up over coffee with a friend.

After singing lessons with her Zeide, Madison will read books with her Bubbie. Next, they all go to the park together, then it's television time in the living room, and they enjoy one another's company. This all while they allow their son to have some me-time. It doesn't go unnoticed. What else doesn't go unnoticed? How they don't try and change you for someone you're not. You know, I never really understood the mindset of some fathers out there who would have done absolutely anything for that child of theirs to make it in pro hockey because they never could, or demand that they take over the family business when it was time to do so.

Other than the money aspect, I ask: Why? Sure, money helps, but it's not the key to happiness, and isn't that what we're all chasing after here? Happiness? I'll tell you what someone once told me, "You know what the problem is with the world these days? We're never happy." That simple question and answer has the ability to challenge you to be the opposite each and every day. And in case you haven't heard this one before, happiness isn't a person, place, or thing, it is a state of mind. So, whether your son or daughter runs the family business, is an accountant, teacher, scientist, DJ, or baker, you be happy for them regardless. It's their health and happiness that are the most important thing, and in turn, if they're happy it should make you happy.

Thankfully my parents gave me the freedom to be able to choose what my passions were and have supported my life and work decisions that have made me happy along the way. They may have not agreed with everything, but they did their best to adapt, and that's all I could ever ask. Be a supportive parent; you won't regret it and they'll never forget where they came from. I know I haven't.

It all began in a townhouse in North York, Ontario. My parents and I lived there. I don't remember any of it as it was only the first couple of years of my life that I was there. Thankfully my folks saved some video footage from our next home, which was another temporary one. As Mom puts it, it was a teardown shack. We were waiting for our new house to be finished. That video footage by the way is on VHS. Don't you think it's about time I converted it to DVD or put it on Youtube? Ya, I'd say so.

Either way, it's saved and something I'm grateful to my parents for having all these years as a keepsake. The years I do remember and am quite fond of are my time spent at my parent's house in Thornhill, Ontario. It's the home they still have today and have now lived in for more than thirty years. We moved in when I was three years old. Dad would often open the door to the garage, push the button for the garage opener, wait until it opened and then he'd holler, "Eric. Robbie. Time for dinner!"

We were the neighborhood kids always out late playing hockey or baseball on the street and the only way we were going inside was when Mom or Dad would call us in for dinner over and over again. By the fourth or fifth attempt we'd finally listen. If it weren't for them calling us in for dinner we would have been out there until who knows when, and of course they didn't want that to happen.

Growing up with Pops was great. He and I would collect baseball and hockey cards in our spare time. And every Friday night after we bought a new pack of cards, we'd pick up a pizza to-go. Friday nights were always pizza nights at our place and I looked forward to them very much every week. What kind of kid wouldn't?

Another one of my hobbies as a kid was making my wrestling action figures fight one another in a toy wrestling ring. I mostly did this on my own; it wasn't really Dad's thing, which was totally understandable. It sure did make a lot of noise though. Mom ended up despising it and regretted even buying it. Guess you could compare her feelings to someone buying a toddler say a drum set or a whistle. The mother of that toddler would not be thrilled with whoever bought that due to all the added noise it would create in a home. The only difference here was, Mom was actually the one who got me the toy wrestling ring as a gift.

Perhaps she thought I'd be quieter with it, which wasn't the case. She asked me to wrestle the action figures in the basement, so there would be less unwanted noise around her. Most of the time I'd listen. Sometimes I wasn't so courteous or I'd forget. I guess you could say Mom learned her lesson in all this, because I don't recall receiving any other gifts from her that caused unwanted noise. In the end I wrestled the action figures so much that the ring cracked and broke in certain parts. That didn't stop me from using it though. When it finally became unusable, it was time for it to be thrown out. Mom was thrilled, and, to her relief, I picked up a new, less noisy hobby.

"Dad, we'll try and leave the park soon, the last one has to be a smacker though! Ok?" I'd say this over and over again to Dad when it came to batting practice at the park when I was a kid. What did it mean exactly? Well, when Dad threw me batting practice, I wanted to make sure I ended off the session on a good note, and a "smacker" meant a line drive, preferably a pulled line drive down the right field line because I was a left-handed hitter at the plate.

I used to absolutely love pulling the ball. Hitting opposite field line drives was fairly challenging for me. Normally I could make it happen if I swung late on a pitch, but to purposely hit the opposite way was something I always had trouble with. Dad and I have bonded regularly over baseball throughout the years, whether it was watching the Toronto Blue Jays at home together, or going to Blue Jays games in downtown Toronto. We were always looking for more and more ways to connect over the game of baseball. He helped make me a better ball player throughout my teenage years by reminding me how important it was to practice, and he helped out a lot with those practices. He even coached me one year. How about driving your son all over the province of Ontario just so he could play baseball growing up? Yup, he did that too. I realize he's not the only one and many parents do this for their children. All I'm saying is I'm thankful for his sacrifice, and hopefully your children are too.

"Robbie, where are we? You've driven us off the beaten track," Mom said. We began to laugh, Mom too because she realized how funny it sounded when she said it. I took a wrong turn while driving my brother and my folks to Montreal from Toronto. The wrong turn landed us in Morrisburg, Ontario. Where? Ya, I hadn't heard of it either until we got lost there one day. It was a small, quiet town. Can't imagine how much a house would cost you out there? You could probably sell a house in Toronto or Vancouver and get two in Morrisburg. Something to really consider if you've had just about enough of the big cities and bright lights.

The tears from laughing so much were rolling down our cheeks and eventually we got back on the 401 headed in the right direction. That's one thing I love about my family; we all have a great sense of humor. Growing up, driving from Toronto to Montreal once a year became a tradition for my mom, dad, brother, and I. We observe the Jewish holiday "Passover" and even though we have many cousins and family members that live in different parts of Canada and the United States, most of our extended family members live in Montreal, so Montreal became this main hub for the entire family to meet up in once per year and catch up.

It got expensive, especially for our West Coast family members, but at the end of the day it's difficult to put a price tag on something that has to do with family. We were approaching the Décarie Expressway, which meant we were about twenty minutes away from our destination in Montreal when Mom said, "Robbie, watch out for that driver!"

Dad followed up with, "Slow down Robbie."

It turns out that a lot of drivers in Montreal don't like to indicate when they're changing lanes. Sure, it happens other places, but Montreal is known for it. Thankfully I didn't collide with the vehicle that cut me off, and, even though I was paying close attention, I still made sure to thank my parents for the heads up. There's no such thing as having too many eyes on the road helping you out when you need it most! As a teenager and still to this day Mom would say, "It's not you I'm worried about Robbie, it's the other drivers."

Feels good to hear that, like a boost of confidence somewhat and a compliment at the same time. We arrived in the Montreal suburb of Outremont at my uncle's place just in time for dinner. Most of our extended family had arrived already. We said our hellos and then it was time to dig into some Chinese food while sharing more laughs, this time around the dinner table.

Most people only publicly acknowledge someone special to them once they've passed on. I want to thank my parents right now, while they're still here, so they can see it. I want them to know how much I love them, and how eternally grateful I am that they gave me life, food, shelter, and water when growing up. It's really all about being thankful for life's simplicities, which to some isn't so simple. My parents gave me the best brother I could ever ask for, and I can easily say that Mom and Dad have been our biggest fans throughout all of life's challenges, obstacles, and wins. If that's not love, I don't know what is.

7

INTERMITTENT FASTING

He looked over at me in the men's change room and jokingly said, "Rob, do you want to lose weight?"

Before I could even finish saying "yes" he replied, "Don't eat." He continued by saying, "All these diet plans ask you to count calorie after calorie, but why would you do that? Just don't eat."

We both laughed because we're both obsessed with keeping weight off, more me than him and I knew he was exaggerating when he said "just don't eat." I think you know what I'm getting at here though. If not, I'll be a little clearer; weight loss, lifestyle, and feeling better about your life than you previously did daily. His name is Ray and he helped better my life by introducing me to intermittent fasting.

Here's the thing, I have a serious obsession about wanting to not be overweight. I'll tell you why, but first, intermittent fasting, also known as I.F., is not so much a diet as it is restricted eating in which you have your meals in a daily timed window of opportunity that's usually between 6-8 hours in length. The rest of the day you fast. Black coffee and water are allowed during your fast. If you want a reformed approach to I.F., add milk or cream and a little bit of sugar to your coffee throughout the fast. There are other forms of the I.F. regimen but the 16/8 (fast for 16 hours/allowed to eat in an 8-hour window each day) is the most common one.

It gives you the opportunity to lose weight while receiving a slew of other health benefits that go along with it. Is it challenging at first? Absolutely. But like any new habit, it takes a couple of weeks to adjust, then once you do, it really becomes like second nature. I.F. has been talked about for quite some time now and is getting more and more popular as time goes on. Ray was someone who caught onto it a few years before it actually became popular.

I can't tell you how grateful I am for the way he introduced me to it. The thing about Ray is, he has such a calm demeanor about him that he really made it easy to take a liking to his approach. I enjoyed his sense of calmness. It felt like there was no pressure at all, which really there wasn't. He said, "Try I.F. Rob. Try eliminating breakfast from your day. Try it for a week. You know what, how's this: try it for a month, and then get back to me. If you're not noticing any results, then go back to your old routine."

I said, "Ok, I'll try it." It turns out I never looked back.

Being hangry is the memory that sticks out most when I first started intermittent fasting. If you're experiencing the same, don't lose hope. Consider drinking a little more coffee than you normally would. This is where being a coffee lover like myself comes in handy. Coffee is an appetite suppressant. So, as long as you're drinking it in moderation, it will help you with your fasting regime. I have found one to two medium sized cups of coffee per day helps. So does water; drink lots of water.

One week into intermittent fasting and I could already notice results. I must have been down at least a couple of pounds. I was stoked. Then a month went by and it's like it was a whole new me. Down ten pounds and a flatter belly too. I made sure to thank Ray. This didn't just happen with the help of intermittent fasting, though. From several years of experience, I can tell you I.F. works best for weight loss when you combine it with high intensity exercise on a regular basis.

What's high intensity? Well, when I was in the best shape of my life, a few years ago, I used to attend spin classes at the gym three to four times a week. A firefighter I know who attends the same gym as me said, "If you cycle three times a week and intermittent fast, you'll be down ten pounds in no time."

Boy was he ever spot on with that. All of a sudden, my family began to notice my weight loss, then people at work started to notice too. This *never* happened to me before. I had never been successful at weight loss. All it took was four weeks. Then the questions came. "Hey Rob, how did you do it?" "What's your weight loss secret?"

At first, I was hesitant to spill the beans, because part of me didn't want the attention. I was hoping people would notice, but a part of me didn't want them to notice. I was conflicted and this was because I had trouble believing the hype of I.F. for fear that it would not work out. I felt like I had been battling weight issues for most of my life, so I wanted this new lifestyle to actually work. I wanted it to be something that would actually have longevity and not just be a fad. Being a superstitious kind of guy, I didn't want to jinx anything by saying too much to anyone too soon. So, I didn't.

Weight has always been a sensitive subject for me. I do try to control this obsession of not wanting to be overweight, but normally I allow the obsession to control me. Maybe that's a good thing? I'm not sure. Over the years I've been made fun of numerous times for being too heavy and it finally got to me emotionally. I don't want a big gut and I think many people out there would say the same for themselves. Perhaps you're one of those people? I mean, don't you want life to feel good? I'm not trying to make this sound like an infomercial here. I'm just trying to be real with you and share how I.F. has benefitted me.

How would you like to add some more clarity to your mind, to your visions, and to your day to day tasks as a whole, all while having to buy new jeans because your old ones are too loose? I'll tell ya, it's a good problem to have! And it's achievable! Listen, being lighter feels better, there's no question.

Now you may say, "Well Rob, it's not so easy." Agreed. There isn't much that's good in life that comes easy, unless you win the lottery, but even then, will that give you eternal happiness and make everything good in life come easy?

Not necessarily.

You have to practice discipline daily when it comes to weight and with that comes flipping the switch in your brain in regards to food if you want to manage your weight well. It's about altering your mindset and it's about being mindful. I'm telling you from experience. For example, instead of playing victim to your appetite when your stomach grumbles a couple hours into your morning routine, own it before your appetite owns you.

Have a coffee instead to suppress the appetite a little. Or, if you don't drink coffee, gulp down that bottle of water. It's important to stay hydrated in order to have an easier fast. Don't be afraid to have your own water bottle at your desk at work at all times. Make it a game for yourself. I often have. I would say to myself, "How far into my day can I go before I really feel like my body needs to be replenished with nutrients? Can I beat yesterday's time? Can I at least tie it?"

Don't be afraid to reward yourself at the end of your fast too. Nobody said what you eat has to be perfect inside the window of opportunity to eat each day in order to drop some weight. So, go ahead, have some chocolate in moderation at the end of one of your meals. If you want to drop more than ten pounds, then obviously you have to monitor yourself more closely and maybe have one piece of chocolate instead of four or five per day.

You can also find other ways of rewarding yourself that won't involve food. As a suggestion, maybe after a long fast, followed by a nutritious meal, you buy yourself that new jacket you've been eying lately or take a weekend getaway somewhere. For less expensive rewards, maybe you get out and embrace nature, spend more time enjoying a hobby, take in a play at a theatre, or a baseball game. Whatever is important to *you*, remember to reward yourself once in a while when you begin succeeding at intermittent fasting and once you become a pro at it too.

In terms of maintaining that flatter gut in life, we must try our best to look at food differently than how we may have been taught to. Presently, I ask myself these two questions: Will this food help get me to the next day feeling satiated? and Is what I'm putting in my body healthy and rich in nutrients for the most part? Nobody's perfect. What you have to understand about intermittent fasting is that you will be hungry at times and when you're outside your window of opportunity to eat, that's when your will power will be tested the most.

Can you sustain yourself? Can you make it to the finish line? You sure can. It takes a little bit of time and some patience, but eventually it'll become like second nature to you. Difficult to imagine now if you're not an intermittent faster, but it's true. Sure, there will be days, mostly weekends I imagine, that you will not stick to your I.F. regimen or you feel pressured to eat certain unhealthy foods that you wouldn't normally eat at family gatherings and such. But as long as you get back on track, back to your regularly scheduled program the next day, or the day after that, you should be ok.

It may take a few days to drop the extra weight you gained throughout the period of time you weren't eating healthy with some cheat meals, but, again, the main thing to remember with I.F. is to get back on the horse if you fall off. I.F. will forgive you if you get back on track; you don't need to feel like you have to give up. You should be able to lose that weight again. Just be mindful and encourage yourself after a cheat meal to get right back to where you originally started. That's the best thing you can do for yourself.

I.F. is almost like learning how to ride a bike in some ways. The more you ride your bicycle the better you become at it. The more you fast the quicker your body adapts. Many of us get way too discouraged and give up easily once we start heading in the wrong direction with a new diet or lifestyle. That's the thing, you don't have to feel that way with I.F., and if you ask me, I.F. isn't really a diet that's going to make you shed pounds all the time. After a few months you might plateau and then I.F. turns into more of a lifestyle than anything else, which in turn will help you feel good daily. And if you do eventually plateau at your weight loss goals with I.F. and don't continue to change up your diet for the better, I.F. can still provide you with that really cool benefit of successful weight management. That's not bad, that's actually really helpful.

Should you decide to try I.F., what you will notice is that there is a lot of reverse psychology involved when it comes to eating, but I want you to know that's perfectly normal. Your mind and body will thank you for it. You can do this, and hey, if you have any doubts, at the very least, it doesn't hurt to try. It doesn't have to be forever if it's not for you.

When I first started I.F. I used to hide what I was doing like it was a big deal even though it wasn't. I mean fasting has been around forever, so it wasn't like it was some sacred secret, but I was indeed hesitant to share my new lifestyle. I think it was because I live with my Italian in-laws and I could sense that what I was about to embark on would be very foreign to them.

In case you were wondering why I live with my in-laws to begin with, it's so that my wife and I can try and save some money for renovations on our own house while we rent it out. Life is expensive, I know! And I'm super grateful to my in-laws for allowing us to invade their retirement life. If I were in their shoes, I would have kicked us out a long time ago. We have a very loud and outgoing, nonstop, never-leaves-you-alone six year old, who is one of the greatest miracles that's ever happened to me. And then there is me, the son in law that uses three towels a week for his showers and piles on the laundry that my mother-in-law doesn't allow me to help out with. Probably for the fear that I'll break something, which I probably would.

In terms of what it was like for my in-laws growing up, it was *very* challenging. They came from an era where an entire family of four would have to split one slice of bread per day and only children were allowed to drink milk, never adults. There just wasn't ever enough. Nowadays my in-laws make sure to make up for that horrible past of theirs by eating thoroughly and nutritiously so that they never have to be reminded of those terrible times in their lives.

That's totally understandable and I respect that, but I had to do what was best for me at the time. I had to try fasting and give it a fair shot too. So, I decided to hide my intermittent fasting regime from my family for a bit, at least for the first month and a half anyway. I really just wanted to see if it would work without anyone bugging me about it or trying to persuade me not to do it. It was easy to hide because I just didn't have breakfast in the morning and I was never usually home during breakfast hours anyway. Eventually my mother-in-law did catch on though.

She noticed I wasn't having some of the lunches she would cook up because I wanted to see if I could fast longer into the day. *Busted.*

My mother-in-law does a lot of cooking for my family and me, and when she wants to feed you, it's usually because she likes you, so liking you and not feeding you doesn't really make any sense to her.

Luckily, with a bit of time, she did get used to me not making any sense to her in the kitchen. She probably just hides her feelings towards it better if you ask me. All good though. That's why I'd never pressure anyone to try intermittent fasting. If three meals a day and snacks work for you, amazing! As I always say, do what works best for you. Now that things were out in the open and I officially felt accepted for my choices, I could breathe a little easier knowing that I no longer had to hide my new diet and lifestyle.

There is a slew of benefits to I.F. other than shedding a few pounds. It provides more mental clarity I find, and you feel more focused even with multiple tabs open in your brain on the daily. It is the ability to function at your highest potential while feeling less sluggish. How about having to know you only have to prepare two meals a day instead of three? That's a bonus. And I.F. is also supposedly very good for your skin. It can also reduce blood pressure, and according to new research it might actually help you live longer.

I'm sure there are more benefits out there that I haven't even read up on yet, and experts continue to do research on it, so who knows what else they could find. What I know as of right now though is, the positives outweigh the negatives. At least for me, anyway. Maybe for you too? What are the negatives? Mostly being hungry and irritable at times due to what some would call extreme hunger, but a lot of that goes away after being on I.F. for a month, and like I've told you before, coffee helps suppress the appetite during your fast.

Also, always drink more water, or as much as you can throughout the day. I can't say that enough. Those methods should help you manage your fast well. I do suggest you consult with your family doctor though before adopting the intermittent fasting lifestyle. Is it for everyone? Absolutely not. There are health conditions that won't allow for this type of fasting. So, be cautious and I encourage you to do your research to find out if it's for you.

Is intermittent fasting a miracle worker in regards to losing weight? From my experience on it, not necessarily, but I do know you can drop a few pounds and then maintain your weight by making it your full-time lifestyle choice. It also depends what kind of foods you put in your body. It isn't rocket science. Put nourishing foods in your body and you will feel better overall, plus your jeans won't feel snug. Make all kinds of unhealthy choices with your food intake and you won't feel as good. You might have to go shopping for new clothes not for the reasons you want to, and chances are it could lead to all kinds of health problems down the road. Everything in moderation. That's how I've mostly lived my life.

You're going to have your cheat meals. The idea is to forgive yourself and get back on track the next day. To say that, when intermittent fasting, you can eat whatever you want all the time inside your window of opportunity to eat each day, would be incorrect. You still have to watch yourself. Sure, you might have a bit of a competitive advantage over someone that's not fasting and not managing their weight well, so you may be able to sneak in your weakness like I do each day without affecting your waistline too much. But for the most part, food needs to be about nourishing the body. I'm human like anyone else and I have certain weaknesses too when it comes to food. It's ok to admit that.

Generally speaking, my weakness is chocolate and certain salty foods. Eventually I have to find a way to eliminate that, but maybe I don't? Maybe I need to live on the edge just a little bit; maybe you do too. That being said, in order to achieve optimal success in more ways than one with I.F. or no I.F., you have to get into the habit of eating to live, not living to eat.

Like most things I've found to be enjoyable in life, I.F. has turned into a bit of an obsession for me. After a few years on the 16/8 I.F. regimen (sixteen hours fasting daily and an eight hour window of opportunity to eat each day), I'm now on a 23:1 window most days and have been for the last year or so. That means roughly twenty three hours of fasting per day and a one hour window of opportunity to eat food. 23 hours of fasting! Daily. Yes, sometimes I'm irritable because of it.

Now, allow me to be up front with you. I gradually got here. It didn't just happen overnight. Your body might need some time to adjust too if you decide to tackle this extreme form of I.F. as well. I went from an eight hour eating window to a six, to four, then came two and eventually one meal a day also known as OMAD. It's not easy and I was never really certain I wanted to do OMAD, now I feel as if I don't have a choice.

Why is that exactly? Why have I taken intermittent fasting to such an extreme? Chronic pain. I used to be able to participate in spin classes three to four times a week burning roughly 430-500 calories per class. I haven't been able to do that in quite some time, so I figure the only way to balance out what's happening with my weight and the lack of participation in high intensity exercise is to do the math. I have to try to consume less calories in a day, so I give myself a smaller time frame to eat while incorporating only moderate exercise in my life right now.

That being said, perhaps I can eventually expand that window of opportunity to eat daily now that I recently received permission from a neurologist at a hospital to ride a bike again and participate in spin class. We shall see. One day at a time, and like I've always suggested to family and friends in life, make sure you do you. Do whatever works best for you, go with that. If I.F. turns out to not be your thing, that's totally ok, but you'll never know unless you try.

Do you want to lose weight? Don't eat.

8

SEASONAL AFFECTIVE DISORDER

I think it's safe to say that each and every one of my fellow Canadians at some point experiences Seasonal Affective Disorder in some form. Our winters can be very long and dark and our summers can be quite unbearably hot. Seasonal Affective Disorder is a type of depression that's related to changes in seasons. It can really begin to take over your life if it isn't managed properly.

If I had to take a guess, and not just because I struggle with this type of Seasonal Affective Disorder, I'd have to say the most common form of it would be having to deal with winter time. This means, that in North America, if you don't live in a warm climate, then November through April is somewhat brutal for you when it comes to the weather and your mood. You're not the only one if that's the case. Trust me on that.

Why do you think there are so many Canadian snow birds that flock down south during those months once they're retired? To get away from the reality of Canada being way too cold, snowy, and dark for far too long. Seasonal Affective Disorder is also known as "SAD" for short and I can't speak for those that deal with SAD throughout spring, fall, or summer, but I can speak about the hardships of our Canadian winters and I'll get to that later on.

First, if you do struggle with SAD during the non-winter months, I urge you to seek help in regards to it, because I myself don't know how to treat and or manage that form of SAD. Talk to your doctor, a friend, or someone else who is going through what you're going through. Be open to getting help from someone you trust is all I could ask. It's important for your overall well-being. My Seasonal Affective Disorder story is an interesting one to say the least. Do I think it could help others on their journey? Absolutely. It's the main reason I want to share it with you.

It all started when I was living in British Columbia in the winter of 2006/2007. I noticed the clouds were a lot puffier in Western Canada than they were out on the East Coast. Perhaps it was because I was living in a valley and that's just what happens when there are no high rise buildings around. I wasn't sure but I became very depressed for how little sunshine I was getting throughout the one winter I was there. When you'd get an overcast day in B.C. it would seem a lot darker than it did back home in Ontario. The clouds would swoop down almost touching Okanagan Lake.

My wife and I would sometimes joke that B.C. really stood for "Big Clouds." I love British Columbia and I'm so grateful I had the chance to live there, but, in all honesty, it felt like I was always out to chase the sunshine when I was outdoors. And when the sun *was* there, it wouldn't stay for long.

I'm not sure if we were there for an off year when it came to the weather? Or maybe I just had higher expectations. One thing I'm fairly certain of is this would be the reason why Vancouver, B.C. is one of the most popular areas to migrate to from the U.K. The climate and the sky are very similar to one another. They both get dark and dreary days for close to eight months out of the year. Some people enjoy that climate, others do not. I was somewhere in the middle. I don't mind a good rain storm or cloudy day here or there, but not for the better part of six to eight months straight.

Do you have a favorite kind of winter day? Mine is one where it's sunny, not a cloud in the sky and somewhere between -5 and -15 degrees Celsius (23 and 5 degrees Fahrenheit). We've been lucky to get many of those over the years in Ontario. I missed that when I was living in beautiful B.C.

The one positive about that winter darkness is that most of the time you're sitting anywhere between 0 to 5 degrees Celsius (32 to 41 degrees Fahrenheit) throughout the day in many parts of British Columbia. So, would you trade sunny, cold winters for mild, gloomy ones? That fellow obviously couldn't. And you know what? At the time I wouldn't have blamed him, but now I have an entirely different outlook on SAD and I truly feel it can be managed to the point where you can live anywhere within reason despite what the weather will be like.

"There goes Rob globe-trotting again," my two best friends wrote in our guys WhatsApp chat a few years ago. They wrote that to me a lot. Understandably so, they were beyond annoyed with my antics. Deep down inside I knew I was going through something emotionally; I just didn't quite understand what.

Globe-trotting meant I'd search many destinations down south on my phone, mostly in Florida, then I would screen shot their forecasts and during one of our Canadian winters a few years ago I'd send these screen shot photos to my friends on a regular basis while telling them how much I wanted to live in those warm and sunny destinations and not here in Canada. I would often tell them that we should all move there due to our long, cold, dreary and snowy winters.

What I was doing was wrong though to be honest, but at the time it didn't seem like it. This is a mental health matter. At the end of the day everything is about mindset and back then mine was a little out of whack. Anywhere there were palm trees, that's where I wanted to be all the time, but life's not all about sunshine and palm trees. There's more to it. We should all be able to live happily wherever we're situated, as long as you have a roof over your head and food on the table. You decide how you're going to feel about any given day no matter the season.

Eventually, embracing winter is what got me out of the funk I was in. It was all thanks to my friend Phil who told me to embrace winter in the first place. I call him Philly, great guy and I'm so thankful that he's my best friend. Soon enough the words "globe-trotting" began to taper off. I was healing and I was grateful. That being said, if I do ever get to retire, I'd love to spend more time down south throughout the winter. I know I can't be the only one.

How do we best manage Seasonal Affective Disorder? Well, for one, always trying to have something to look forward to throughout the year helps, especially if you struggle with SAD during the winter months. Having something to look forward to is something we as Canadians need due to how hard we work. Let's be honest, many of us put in quite a few hours at the office or on a job site. So, in November you have the holidays coming up the following month, that's something to look forward to and then I think it's really important to try and get away in the new year or sometime in the winter, preferably down south for a week so you can get some natural vitamin D on you. It's healthy for the mind, body, and soul.

You understand that a vehicle needs an oil change every few months, well your mind and body need the same. Another method to help cope with SAD is something I touched on earlier, being able to really try your best to embrace winter or whichever season you're having difficulty with by just getting outside and playing around in it. That could mean making a snowman with your children, having a snowball fight, forcing yourself to go for a walk all bundled up when it's minus twenty out and bicycle riding through a bunch of leaves on a trail in the fall. There's also vitamin D supplements; don't forget about those.

Along with trying my best to embrace winter, I have certainly found vitamin D supplements to help cope with SAD. Vitamin D is known as the sunshine vitamin. If you're really feeling the effects of the dreary weather throughout winter, then a higher dose of vitamin D supplements might be recommended to you. Consult with your doctor first to find out how much vitamin D you should be taking daily. There are also light therapy lamps, which are worth looking into as well.

Everything in life is about management, including SAD, and if you've got a lot of money, then it's easy to manage. Simply buy or rent property wherever the weather is best for you. For most of us though, that's not an option, so I certainly hope this advice helps you live your best life despite what Mother Nature provides outside your front door.

9

KEEP DREAMING - DEDICATED TO THE FIELD OF DREAMS MOVIE SITE IN DYERSVILLE, IOWA

What's the point of having a dream, chasing it and then having it come true? You might say self-fulfillment and happiness, but I think greater than that it gives our lives purpose. I've always believed that having to work in a profession you absolutely despise is not something you should do by choice. Have to do it just to get by? Then sure, but always be on the lookout for something that is more fulfilling and more up your alley.

I can't tell you how upsetting it is to me to have seen all these adults over the years on public transit look like they are absolutely miserable going to and coming home from their nine to five. It might be for good reason that they're unhappy, and if so, I certainly sympathize, but I could tell that the majority were the ones out in the workforce most likely finishing up with slaving away at another day. Let me ask you this: If you love what you do for a living, is winning the lottery all that it's chalked up to be? I don't think it is to be honest. Sure it helps, but part of me thinks that's why I haven't played the lottery all that much.

Money won't make you happy, but your state of mind will. Think about it, wouldn't all these multimillion-dollar professionals in the world just stop what they're doing and hit the beach for the remainder of their days? Nope, because they love what they do and they need to find ways to try and keep their minds busy. I'm beyond grateful to be one of the lucky ones who can honestly say that for most of my professional life I've worked all kinds of jobs that I've had a passion for. Those opportunities made me, and continue to make me, so appreciative. That didn't just happen overnight though. It all started with a dream and then I kept dreaming. You also have to have the proper vision for those dreams, along with the right plan. Then you have to work incredibly hard at chasing those dreams, and when you finally see them come to fruition, you'll realize that dream fulfillment is one of the best feelings you could have ever imagined, money aside.

Here's how I would describe the feeling of fulfilling a dream: It's like being a kid in a candy store. Dream fulfillment is that feeling of satisfaction inside like no other. If your eyes could light up like a Christmas tree, they would. Your heart is warmed and your spirit is ignited. I imagine it's good for your mental health to some degree too, and I think having a challenge from time to time keeps us feeling more alive.

After fulfilling one dream, you want to dream some more, and there's nothing wrong with that. I do it all the time actually. Some dreams are realistic, and others might have to stay just that, a dream. But the more you chase those realistic dreams, the more fulfilling your life will be.

Some of the most fascinating dreams I put the work in to fulfill over the years have had to do with baseball and radio. Aside from my family and friends, those are my two greatest passions in life. It all started with a vision, and I made sure to try and take the appropriate steps of action to fully understand what my dreams were before actually chasing them. A lot of that had to do with writing things down word for word. I've always been a fan of that. It's what my dad taught me. He'd say, "Rob, when life gets overwhelming, just mark what you have to do down on a sheet of paper." So, that's what I often did. You might find that beneficial too. Just mark it down.

Have you heard of the movie Field of Dreams? It's a classic

from 1989, filmed in Iowa. A film about baseball, relationships, and redemption. It's my favorite movie of all time. Perhaps yours too? Well, get this, one day I put my name in the hat for a contest online with the Field of Dreams movie site. It was the opportunity to win a gift card to the movie site's gift shop, except the only reason I entered the contest in the first place was to see if someone would actually respond to me and possibly offer me some kind of work opportunity at the field if I handed in my resume.

It turned out I won the contest, and I told Roman, the operations manager at the Field of Dreams, that I wasn't interested in retrieving the gift card and that he could either donate it to charity or give it to someone else that's also a massive Field of Dreams fan.

Roman was shocked. He couldn't believe I wanted to do that.

I said, "Instead of receiving the gift card, do you mind if I send you my resume? I have interest in somehow doing work for you, whether that's remotely done or in person at the field in Iowa."

He asked about my background and I told him it was mainly in broadcasting.

He goes, "Alright, sure. Send me your resume and audio samples and we'll go from there."

It was amazing. I couldn't believe it. From winning a gift card to potentially getting the opportunity to work at the Field of Dreams movie site. The next thing I knew I was talking to the ops manager (Roman) at the field about hosting Military Appreciation Day *live* at the Field of Dreams movie site because he really took a liking to my demos and resume. Military Appreciation Day was going to be a day dedicated to the families and members of the U.S. Military past and present and to raise money on their behalf.

Roman made me the voice of the official commercial for Military Appreciation Day at the field as well which would air on several radio stations in the mid-western part of the United States. Then, it all came together. Flight arrangements, accommodations, and the opportunity to be the PA guy, MC and play-by-play fella at the Field of Dreams movie site on June 1st, 2019. What a thrill!! I hadn't dreamt about working at the Field of Dreams for a very long time, but nonetheless it was still a vision I had that became a dream for a short period of time, and eventually it all came true thanks to the wonderful operations manager at the Field of Dreams.

I think he could tell how big of a fan I was of the movie. I wasn't just an ordinary fan; I mean when you can recite the lines to several scenes in the movie it brings you to that next level in terms of fandom.

I'm telling you all of this because you can do this with how it relates to some of your own interests in life too. All it really takes is a little bit of time, vision, patience, and authentic excitement for what you're about to try and achieve. Be nice to everyone you meet too and take mental note of the ones who don't reciprocate that back to you as you climb the ladder to the top.

June 1st, 2019 arrived. I remember waking up super early that morning because I was too excited to sleep. Roman drove me to the actual movie site in Dyersville at about 8am. When we arrived, I made sure to take in how peaceful it was. Sort of like the calm before the storm with roughly two hundred people expected to attend Military Appreciation Day later on that morning.

I noticed the birds were chirping around me, the field, and the farmhouse, just like they did in the movie. Everything I started to see I began to relate to the film. The only time I had been to the field prior to this weekend opportunity was eighteen years ago. It was really nice to be back, and this time it was extra special because I got to go there three days in a row, which really gave me more time to soak it all in. If you're looking for a place to meditate, I tell ya, the field is a great place for it. There's a sense of peace and tranquility to it like no other.

Roman brought me up to his office, which was formerly Ray and Annie's bedroom, located on the top floor in the farmhouse, next to the field. Of course, I took pictures of practically everything in that farmhouse. Would you expect anything less from the guy that could practically recite the movie's lines word for word? Field of Dreams obsessed is what you could call it.

Roman gave me the outline for Military Appreciation Day on paper, along with several sponsor mentions. I remember feeling incredibly grateful and excited when I saw my name on that manuscript for the first time right next to the Field of Dreams movie site logo. It read something like; "Host: Rob Daniels, Military Appreciation Day, June 1st, 2019, Field of Dreams Movie Site, Dyersville, Iowa." Too cool! Just seeing that was a dream in itself fulfilled. Next I had to completely fulfill the dream opportunity at hand, host Military Appreciation Day and do my best to do a darn good job at it too.

"Rob, come on over here," Roman said when we were minutes away from kicking off Military Appreciation Day. He was pointing to the stage. It was time to try and shine. I began to walk towards the stage feeling very confident and fulfilled with what was going on all around me. Stage life is the best life. I love it. I really do. Whether it's to host an event, getting people stoked for their weekend at a nightclub, or hosting shows on multiple platforms. There's a certain over-the-top thrill to it. If you love the spotlight on stage too then you probably know what I mean. I reached over for the microphone at the podium and the next thing you know, it was go time.

First, to welcome everybody to the Field of Dreams movie site in beautiful Dyersville, Iowa. Next, why we were here. To gather in support of and to honor the American Military. There was a twenty-one-gun salute I had to introduce followed by the singing of the American national anthem. What an honor just to be there. I love America for how patriotic they are. Hearing the twenty-one-gun salute gave me goose bumps. *Wow*, I thought. This was everything I had ever dreamed it would be and more. When it came time to thank the sponsors and organizers of the event, well, that's when I started to tear up.

Tears were rolling down my face and I choked up when thanking Roman for bringing me out to heaven, a.k.a. the Field of Dreams movie site to host this wonderful event. It really was a dream come true for me in heaven. From being the MC, to the PA guy and play-by-play personality all at the one place that as early as my childhood, inspired and taught me to live my life as a dreamer. It was fulfilling a dream at the iconic grounds where it was instilled in my brain that if I had enough passion and perseverance, I could fulfill any dream if I put my mind to it.

Thankfully even with my emotions running wild, I made it through my introduction speech and the sponsorships. Roman and some of the other event organizers came over to me afterwards to thank me for my work on stage and to let me know just how appreciative they were about my passion towards the game of baseball in America and the Field of Dreams. Next up was a Little League game at the Field Of Dreams followed by members of the American Military taking on several local folks from Dubuque County in a softball game under the lights. Now, if only we could slow time down just a little? With everything in me I continued to try and savor each moment of being at that field.

There was a lawn chair set up for me down the right field line. I had the wireless microphone in hand, to my right was the dead Iowa corn, which was considered homerun territory, and to my left a great view of the field as the little leaguers were about to begin their game. Nowhere in my deal with Roman was it outlined that I'd be calling the play-by-play for the little league game. He was just nice enough to give me the extra experience of calling a game at the world-famous Field of Dreams movie site. This dream was only getting better and better as time went on. All I could do was relish in it. I knew this day and weekend in Iowa wasn't going to last forever, so I continued to try and savor every moment.

Keeping things fun and entertaining on the microphone was and is how I work best. Besides, it was a Saturday, you could tell everybody was out there to enjoy a good time while supporting a great cause. I've never been all that funny though over the years with my time on the microphone, but I have been creative. which has brought out a giggle or two from time to time, including one remark I made at the field that afternoon when a foul ball was hit in the air towards the farm house.

It ended up landing on the farm house roof, to which I said something along the lines of, "And the pitch; fouled off in the air towards the farm house and that one lands on the roof, right on top of Ray and Annie's bedroom." If you've seen Field of Dreams, you most likely know approximately where Ray and Annie's bedroom is located in that farmhouse. Hearing the spectators laugh totally made my day. It was amazing.

The little league game had wrapped and before the spectators at the event could take in some live music at the field, they grabbed some grub over at several of the local food vendor carts that were on hand for the day. Introducing the musical guests on stage was the easy part, and they were all so gifted at their craft, but I was anxiously awaiting being the PA and play-by-play guy that night for the American Military guys and their softball game under the lights. I did my best to live in the moment though, continuing to just be thankful for being at the field while looking around me and visualizing certain scenes from the movie.

There was Doc. Graham saving Karen's life next to the famous bleachers that still sit next to the field, then I looked over at the mound and visualized myself as Ray Kinsella pretending to pitch BP. It was all so surreal. How did I get to be so lucky? I was reminded again of how it all went down and Roman will always be at the top of my list of people to thank. For if it wasn't for Roman, I would have never been standing in heaven that weekend. This is why I say to chase those dreams of yours, the ones that make sense for your life, because the feeling of dream fulfillment makes life way more worth living. I believe it's good for one's mental well-being too. So, this is where I ask, what are you waiting for? We are not promised tomorrow. Enjoy the chase of tackling whatever it is that ignites the fire inside of you to get up in the morning and live instead of just exist. The only thing standing in your way is you.

"Ladies and gentlemen, girls and boys, here's the starting lineup for the American Military!" What a feeling to finally be able to say that on the PA at Field of Dreams. It was like being chosen as the winner of one of those national singing competitions.

"We believe you have what it takes so instead of receiving your record deal, here's your airline tickets, accommodations and the opportunity to rock the mic at the world-famous Field of Dreams in Dyersville, Iowa, all while receiving some professional exposure in the U.S. as well." Thankful? Yes, extremely. I like to think of it more as eternally grateful for Roman. I can't say his name enough.

If you do visit the field at some point, you'll likely see him either taking care of the grounds on a tractor or perhaps working away in his office if you glance up at some of the windows of the farmhouse. He also is a firm believer of helping out guided tours of the farmhouse when he can, or visiting the newly added merchandise/apparel store along with helping out at the new restaurant on the field grounds, which apparently has some really good food.

Roman made some announcements throughout the Military game, thanking the sponsors and organizers of the event. He was great on the mic and had an incredible customer service approach with the fans at the field as well. It's probably why he's in the line of work he's in.

We were about halfway through the game. It was really nice to see the American Military guys having such a wonderful time on the diamond. That's what it was all about anyway. We were there for them and to celebrate them. The sun began to set and I swear I had never seen anything like it before. Well maybe I had, but this one was extra special because it was in heaven at Field of Dreams. What a sunset!

The backdrop to this field was absolutely stunning around the dinner hour. I mean you have this sensational sunset and a perfect ball diamond. All that was missing was for my family to be there to share in the moment, especially Dad. Oh, and for the corn to be alive too, that would have been the icing on the cake. We were about four weeks out from corn growth. Iowans say the corn grows knee high by the fourth of July. It was June 1st. Never have I seen the corn alive there in person before. Which gives me another good reason to try and get back there one day, right?

Dad really needs to see this place, I thought. We had bonded over the movie for years. Visiting the field has to be a bucket list item for him, and I'd especially love it if my brother and I were there with him in person when he goes for the first time. This way, hopefully we could all have a catch. Imagine that? Catch with Dad and his two sons at the field that inspired us to have a catch with Dad whenever we could, for all these years now. Hopefully one day, hopefully one day.

"Strike three!" the umpire yelled. The guys played a seven-inning game instead of nine. The Military Appreciation Day softball game under the lights had come to an end, but the night wasn't over just yet.

Is there truly anything better than sitting in the outfield at the Field of Dreams movie site while watching the actual movie Field of Dreams on a big screen projector while sipping on a cold one? You don't have to answer that. It might not be your dream, but it certainly was mine. Luckily, I got to fulfill that after the Military Appreciation Day softball game under the lights had ended, and you know what? It was like living a dream within a dream. They actually show the movie often at the field.

What I'd recommend is, if you and your dad want to go to the field sometime, you might be able to pull off a catch at the field, dinner close by, and the showing of the movie Field of Dreams at the iconic Field of Dreams movie site itself. Certainly, call ahead of time or go online to retrieve information on when or if they're planning on showing the film at the site while you're in town, and if you can make it happen, great! If not, it's well worth trying again the next time you visit.

I recall being too fidgety when watching the movie on the outfield grass because I wanted to spend more time in the farmhouse and facetime my wife so she could see some of what was inside. It was my last night in town, so this was essentially my last chance to show her the inside of the farmhouse. I moved myself into the farmhouse and I called her while drinking my cold American lager. When she answered the facetime, I could see and then hear my five-year old being super loud in the background, it was all good though. It was Saturday night! Perhaps she had too much chocolate that night? I wasn't entirely sure, but it sure seemed like it.

My kid always knows how to rope her fellow family members into giving her chocolate, especially me. What can I say, she's Daddy's girl and sometimes she's got me wrapped around her finger. Eventually that will change, I hope. I ended up wandering over to the staircase in the farmhouse to show them to my wife. "Look Mar, the staircase Ray and Annie used when they realized they had the same dream of being at Fenway Park."

She smiled, then said, "Awesome!" and tried to confirm my flight times home for the next day while attempting to get her words across clearly over Madison's singing in the background. I finally comprehended what she was trying to say, and I could tell it was too busy and too loud on her end in order for me to properly show her and explain to her more of what was in the farmhouse over Facetime, so we decided I'd save the stories for when I got home. In the meantime, I needed to think of another way I could soak up the feeling of being at the field a little longer before it was time to leave. I didn't really have many pictures of the field at night, so that's when I started taking all kinds. I'm so happy with how they turned out too and will definitely be developing them someday to put in my own man cave.

You've heard the saying, "All good things come to an end," right? This experience was about to be one of them. I was sad, happy, and all kinds of emotions wrapped into one, but I think most importantly I was so grateful for it all. Roman was super kind to me all weekend, he even ended up driving me back to the airport in Cedar Rapids, Iowa. We said our goodbyes and promised one another that we'd stay in touch. Roman also said to message him when I got home. He wanted to make sure I arrived safely. I thought that was really nice of him. His whole family was nice actually.

I met his young boy who had the blondest hair I'd ever seen on a child. It was spectacular. He had crystal blue eyes too. I mean he could easily be one of those baby models you see online or in a magazine. The kid is going to be a heartbreaker when he grows up, that's for sure. Roman's vehicle slowly drove off from the passenger drop off area at the airport and that's when it sunk in. The dream trip to the corn in Iowa had concluded, but you know what? It set the tone for more dreams to thankfully come true later that summer, and they weren't just my dreams either.

Dad has been a fan of the Toronto Blue Jays for as long as I can remember, which is a very long time. Probably close to thirty years actually. So, throughout the summer of 2019, which was also the summer of the 30th anniversary of the film Field of Dreams, I thought to myself, *What better way to celebrate Father's Day then to have a catch with Dad on our Field of Dreams in Toronto where the Blue Jays play?*

So many dreams had come true for us on that field in Toronto, like the bat flip game, the World Series win in 1993, and a game I have a very vivid memory of. It was a weekend afternoon in Toronto. I was ten years old at most; Dad and I were sitting in the five hundred level down the right field line at what was then called SkyDome. The roof was rolled back and the sun was beaming down on us in the late afternoon as the game had gone into extra innings. The Blue Jays were tied 6-6 with the Yankees, and in exciting fashion Toronto pulled off the victory.

My dad and I were on cloud nine. I'll never forget that feeling of not only excitement in the stadium but how Dad and I were really bonding over this team. It certainly was amazing father/son time every chance we got to watch the Jays together, and it still is to this day. I figured this opportunity for him to step foot on the MLB field in Toronto and throw the ball around with his two sons for a little while would make for an epic Father's Day gift. I had a hunch that this idea of us playing catch on the field we saw so many dreams come true on would ignite that dream come true feeling for him deep down inside. All we needed was five minutes on that field with him and I think he would have been more than satisfied. Luckily, after pulling a few strings, I was able to get my dad, brother, and myself on the field after a Blue Jays game the day after Father's Day in 2019 and it went just as planned. My brother and I couldn't have hoped for anything better.

The roof was still open, and it was after a night game too. The lights were still on in the stadium and we ended up throwing the ball around. Thankfully we took some pictures too. Dad was in heaven. Just like a certain ghost player that discovered the Field of Dreams for the first time. Dad wore my grey Field of Dreams hoodie while I wore my classic Blue Jays 1993 World Series Champions tea-shirt. My brother had some new Blue Jays gear on. The moment couldn't have been more perfect.

You see, you don't necessarily have to chase your own dreams to feel good inside throughout life. Dig deep and truly try to find what life means to someone else and once in a while chase those dreams for them while surprising them too. Remember, a lot about life is how you make someone feel. They might not necessarily remember what you said or did in your life, but the feeling you give someone is different. They'll remember that, trust me. Now go make someone's day by trying to help fulfill their dream! Amen.

It was really fascinating how the dots connected within a thirty-day time frame. From getting to host an event at the Field of Dreams movie site in Dyersville, Iowa to the retrieval of Field of Dreams 30th anniversary celebration audio from top baseball personnel including a hall of famer in St. Mary's Ontario at the Canadian Baseball Hall of Fame. They all wished the Field of Dreams movie site a happy 30th anniversary.

Next, I was trying to fulfill another dream by visiting Buffalo, New York with the hopes of meeting Dwier, who played John Kinsella in the film Field of Dreams. He played Ray Kinsella's dad in the movie. He acted in one of the most popular scenes in movie history if you ask me. The scene where Ray asked him to have a catch. The ultimate dream for me would have been to get a picture of myself and my dad along with Dwier and Ray with baseball gloves on pictured at home plate with the Field of Dreams and the corn as the backdrop. What was about to happen was the next best thing and I was more than alright with that. I was delighted actually.

My wife dropped me off at the ballpark in Buffalo early that day while she went shopping. I had a media credential because Roman back in Iowa gave me access to the Field of Dreams movie site's Instagram page. He suggested an Instagram takeover in Buffalo, showcasing John Kinsella's appearance. *So cool,* I thought. That media credential gave me access to the field where Dwier was hanging out before his public signing in the concourse.

I wasn't shy to introduce myself and take five minutes of his time to let him know just how much the movie meant to me. He was grateful and could tell I was getting emotional. We hugged and then he offered me the opportunity of a lifetime. He asked for me to pick up my glove off the grass so that he and I could have a catch. I was blown away! We ended up throwing the baseball around on that beautiful field in Western New York mimicking the final scene from Field of Dreams just like my dad and I did about two weeks earlier in Toronto. Amazing. It's those kind of moments in life that I'll smile at every time I look back on them.

The concourse at the stadium in Buffalo was packed with people. Most of them were in line to meet Dwier, take a picture with him, and get his autograph. It was amazing to see the turn out, me being one of those fans of course, but working at the same time. Behind the autograph table Dwier was sitting at was a rolled-out poster backdrop of him as John Kinsella from Field of Dreams. It was that famous shot of him taking off his catcher's mask and smiling while wearing his New York Yankees classic uniform. Dwier had a stack of photos of himself in eight by tens that he was ready to sign for fans that were eager to meet him. I was trying my best to calm the kid-in-the-candy-store feeling inside me while taking photographs of Dwier for the Field of Dreams movie site's Instagram page.

Dwier promised me an autograph too, but I wanted to be professional about it and let as many fans as possible meet him first. When my time had come to step up to the autograph table I smiled and thanked him again for that once in a lifetime experience of having a catch with him earlier that day. He took the baseball I wanted signed by him out of the small cardboard box it was in. I asked if he could sign the sweet spot for me. The sweet spot in case you didn't know, is the middle of the baseball, the narrowest area between the stitches. Autographs on baseballs are typically more valuable if they're on the sweet spot.

Dwier agreed to sign the sweet spot, but he also wanted to know if he could add something to it as well. He said, "Do you trust me?"

I said, "Sure."

So, he signed the sweet spot and added the inscription "Go The Distance." That's one of the famous lines the voice whispered to Ray Kinsella in the movie Field of Dreams.

I smiled and then asked, "Ok but what's that supposed to mean? Go the distance?"

He said, "I can't tell you what it means, use it for how it best suits your life." My mind started to race. What on earth could that mean? I tried my best not to think about it any longer that night and instead just embrace where I currently was, which was a beautiful stadium where I was about to take in a baseball game with the amazing John Kinsella.

My wife and I were in a press box at Sahlen Field. Boy, did we ever feel like we were VIP. Food and drinks were on the house and we got to hang out with Dwier. That was the best part. Dwier agreed to an interview with me for multi-platform content creation purposes and my wife was thrilled when he asked her if she wouldn't mind fixing his hair for the video interview. She'd called him a silver fox to me on a couple of occasions. I didn't mind. As someone of the same sex I have no problem at all admitting that Dwier is a very good-looking guy.

Thankfully he was good at answering my questions too. There's nothing worse than conducting an interview with someone that doesn't want to be there. He wanted to be there and he was very candid with his responses to my questions. We talked about his minor-league stadium tour that he was on, and of course the famous role that he's well known for in the last scene of Field of Dreams. He got emotional when talking about that because his dad died not so long before he landed the role and his role would be to play a father that had come back from the dead to make a truce with his son and to, of course, have a catch.

Every single moment of that interview I was incredibly grateful for. Time is precious and knowing how much this movie meant to me I didn't want the interview to end, but it did, and you know what, it went well, so well that at the end of the game Dwier told me to stay in touch, which I have from time to time on Instagram. He even included a photo of he and I in a post on his Instagram shortly thereafter and it made me tear up. The post is from July 18, 2019. The game had ended and my time with Dwier was up. My wife and I along with our two friends walked over towards the car in the parking lot about a block or two away from the stadium in Buffalo. That was it, time to get back on the road and head home. What an experience though. I literally lived the dream with that one! Now, to find out what "Go The Distance" meant.

The first week of July had arrived and I had to start thinking about what I was going to do for my wife's milestone birthday. She was born on the 4th of July. What are the odds? This needed to be a big day for her, a gift card, flowers, or going to the movies wasn't going to be enough this time around. I was sitting in the basement at my in-laws' doing some work on my laptop one day when I looked over at the baseball that Dwier signed for me. I kept staring specifically at the inscription on the ball. "Go The Distance."

My mind was racing again, but this time I think I figured it out. One of my wife's dreams is to get a tour of the bedroom that sits atop of Cinderella's castle at Walt Disney World. I thought, *What are the chances I can make that dream come true for her? Or at least get as close to it as possible?*

Marilena is a huge fan of Disney, but she hasn't had the opportunity to visit the inside of the castle yet. So "Go The Distance" meant go to Florida and attempt fulfilling this dream for her. I was going to do everything in my power to try and get her a tour of that bedroom in the castle, so I made a phone call. A customer service agent told me it was close to impossible to get a tour of the bedroom, you had to be a celebrity and perhaps pay millions to make it happen. I wasn't a celebrity and I didn't have millions, still don't, so settling for the next best thing was all I could really do. The plans had been made; I was to have lunch with my wife inside Cinderella's castle in a couple weeks with Disney characters hanging out in the dining room with us. We were going to Disney World! I couldn't wait to tell her.

Marilena's friend and I organized a surprise birthday party for her at a restaurant with all her family and friends. That's where I got to tell Marilena she was going to Disney in hopes that she would be touching her dream, and who knows, maybe even fulfilling it entirely as well. At that point we didn't know what could happen, especially if we were walking around the theme park all day with me gloating about how it was her birthday trip. Anything is possible and luckily, she was on cloud nine when I told her where she would be going in the next couple of weeks.

Everything turned out well inside Cinderella's castle for lunch that day. We were overlooking the theme park and Marilena was glowing every time a new Disney character welcomed us to lunch at our table. We didn't get to see the bedroom at the top of the castle, but we did see enough for Marilena to say she fully enjoyed the trip, and I think that's what counts here. A happy wife is a happy life is what most people say, and I couldn't agree more. Marilena touched her dream, she didn't quite fulfill it, but hey, maybe one day. Never say never. And you see, this is what helps make life worth living.

Having a vision, a goal, or a dream not only for yourself but for somebody else you care about too. Then you put that information from your vision down on paper if you have to, put the dream together, chase it and then do everything in your power to achieve it. Sometimes you win when you chase those dreams of yours, sometimes you don't. That's life. The key is to not lose hope and if you feel it's right, try again. Remember, fear kills more dreams than failure ever will.

The reality is not every dream is going to make sense for your life. I've chased many dreams for over twenty years now, and my wife has moved to different cities and regions in Canada to be by my side while I fulfilled those dreams. My parents have been super supportive too of my dreams, along with my good friends. I do try to come to terms with myself that in some scenarios a dream will have to stay a dream. A wish will have to stay a wish. Just like Doc. Graham suggested about his dream to Ray Kinsella in his office in the movie Field of Dreams, and that's perfectly ok. Always know that you can modify those dreams of yours if need be and create new, more realistic and achievable dreams too! The sky is the limit. Just because a few dreams and goals that you had didn't work out, doesn't mean you can't fulfill the other ones you have. Another piece of advice if I may, you're never too old to set another goal or to dream a new dream.

10

MY BROTHER THE BLESSING

"It's all mine . . . and yours!" I'd say to Eric, also known as "Pric." He's the furthest thing from a prick actually, but when I was a teenager, I used to spell his name with a P at the beginning instead of an E just to purposely try and get on his nerves, and boy did it ever work. Eric's my younger brother and only sibling. Love him to bits. Most of the time "It's all mine . . . and yours" meant something was given to him and I'd want whatever was given to him too, so with a great deal of exaggeration and emphasis I'd say whatever was given to him was all mine, then I'd pause for a few seconds, and eventually say to him that it was his too. Almost sounding like, "Hey ya, I guess you could have some of it too."

He hated when I did that. We would then begin to argue and Mom would normally break it up by raising her voice at us from upstairs. With age comes maturity though, to most anyway, and in my late teens I stopped teasing my brother. We're both in our thirties now and sometimes we look back on this together and can't help but to laugh out loud. I was incredibly silly and sometimes I still am. Thankfully he continues to put up with me.

The age gap between Eric and I is roughly six years. I was born in December of 1983 and he was born in October of 1989. We shared a lot of the same interests growing up and still do. Baseball being one of them. We went to *a lot* of Blue Jays games together when we were kids. I imagine it was almost a blessing in disguise for my mother. She knew we liked to live at the ballpark on weekends mostly, so that would get us out of her hair for quite a while. When you become a parent, you really begin to understand how important that extra me-time can actually be for your overall wellbeing. After Blue Jays games, Eric and I would continue to find ways of still hanging out. It was either watching movies, playing baseball around the house, or wrestling.

He was really good at wrestling. Being the older brother, I'd sometimes let him win, but a lot of the time I found him to actually be incredibly strong. Stronger than me and I'd tap out frequently. When we were bored, that's when the silliness kicked in. I can't imagine the weird photos we would have taken of one another if selfies existed in our teenage years. One example of our immaturity was that we used to walk into one of the bathrooms in my parent's house, look into the mirror and start making all kinds of weird faces. We called that "the mirror" and we'd often stop and drop whatever we were doing just to do "the mirror." It was really funny, to us anyway. It helped bond us even more, and laugh too. Laughter is always good.

Normally an older brother is supposed to act like an older brother. Always offering up advice, lending a helping hand and providing a support system like no other. I do try my best in playing those roles, but a lot of the time I feel like those roles are reversed. Eric is an incredible individual to confide in. He's been there for me through thick and thin. We've talked relationships, writing, anxiety, health and fitness, chronic pain and more. I respect his outlook on life and that's why I've continued to confide in him over the years. I want him to know he can always reach out to me for advice like I have done with him over the years. He would never be a bother. I think that's what's great about having a sibling.

Say you have a fantastic relationship with them, chances are you'll always have that person to reach out to for help in more ways than one. The more people on your side, the better. You may even think of it as that sibling sometimes becomes another psychologist for you, only this one would be outside of your psychologist's office, doesn't charge an hourly fee, and will most likely be a friend for life.

One summer Eric went to Israel and it's as if he came home a new man. He never really followed conservative Jewish rituals much as a child or teenager, but that all changed a few years back when he became inspired on a trip to the holy land. He now keeps Shabbat every Friday, celebrates the high holidays, which he always has, but now he follows the nonreligious ones too and has an entirely new outlook on religion.

I admire him for it. I don't know if I could practice all the rituals he does, but I'm grateful he teaches me some of what he's learned during Shabbat dinner when my family and I join him from time to time. He's a mensch. I'll save you the google search. A mensch is a person of integrity, and honor and in case you knew that already I apologize if you think I'm insulting your intelligence. I'm not. That's not the only thing that's changed in Eric's life recently, he's also gone vegan. And, in April of 2019, he introduced me to the newest member of our family. That's when Eric became a dad.

Lielle is her name. Like most new parents, they wanted their privacy for a couple of weeks before anyone came to visit the baby, which was totally understandable. I was so anxious though. I really wanted to meet her! When what felt like forever in terms of time passing by had finally ended, I got to meet my niece for the very first time and boy oh boy what a feeling it was.

I was an uncle to my brother's kid, wow. *Unbelievable,* I thought. I was over-the-moon happy for him and his wife. To see how Lielle was lighting up his life made me light up inside. Him and his little fam jam reside in the Greater Toronto Area. We help one another out with dad advice all the time, and I'm a better person for knowing him. To my brother! The incredible family member and friend. I love you Eric.

11

ANXIETY, OBSESSION & DEPRESSION

I knew there was something wrong, but I couldn't quite figure it out. Questioning, wondering, and worrying. Was the door to the car locked? Perhaps I should double or maybe triple check that I locked the front door? What was happening to me? I was maybe fifteen at the time, so Mom took me to a therapist through Jewish Family Services. I was grateful something like this existed, however, I attended maybe two sessions at most. I believe the therapist thought I no longer needed anymore sessions at the time and that I could manage on my own moving forward. I luckily did manage on my own, until I was about 24.

Crying bursts, questioning everything under the sun, sweaty palms, and trouble sleeping. You could say that those would certainly be symptoms of anxiety. I remember specifically looking into the mirror one day in the bathroom in our apartment in Montreal. My eyes were watering from so much crying. I thought to myself, *Why can't I just stop crying?* I felt so weak although the saying goes, sick not weak. You may have heard of the expression "walking on egg shells" before? I was doing that and then some.

They say in any given year, 1 in 5 people in Canada will personally experience a mental health problem or illness. I was certainly one in five in 2008 and 2009. With most anxiety though, there is usually a trigger that tends to make things worse, potentially sending you spiraling, and it can even have the ability to make the anxiety crippling. For some, that trigger is getting on a plane and flying, for others it's a fear of needles or pointed objects, and for others it could be something entirely different.

For me it's being around other people who can't seem to manage their own anxiety in front of me, who make me sweat the small stuff, and are usually high strung in nature when they speak in regards to the pettiest of things. If there's one thing I could try and hammer into your brain it's to please, please, pretty please try and *not* sweat the small stuff, and it's all small stuff. Remember that. What crippled me mentally and emotionally was that I revealed a personal detail to someone regarding a friend without that friend's permission. She did tell me not to tell anyone this, so I felt like I needed to own up to my mistake.

That being said the other person did pressure me a little to reveal the secret. I should have never given into that pressure though. Let's just say the voice that was raised at me turned into more yelling than anything else because I'd argue back that revealing this secret wasn't a big deal, but it was a big deal to her. Now you might think rightfully so that I was yelled at, but sometimes we don't know the extent of damage that can possibly have on a person, and for me, well it caused *a lot* of damage. Mental health damage that is.

It took my anxiety to new heights, and at the time I didn't even fully understand what anxiety was. I instantly became a student of it, I'll tell you that much. I have since forgiven this friend that raised their voice at me and they have forgiven me for revealing their secret, but the next seven months took a toll on my mind big time, they would turn out to be the most challenging seven months of my entire life.

Marilena and her mom left for Cuba in November of 2008 to go and scope out the hotel and resort that Mar and I would later marry at in May of 2009. Marilena left the apartment often when we lived in Montreal, and for good reason, mostly for business purposes, to see family, and to plan our wedding in Toronto. It gave me a better understanding as to what loneliness was really all about.

Don't think that just because you might be single that that is the only type of loneliness that exists. It's not. It is probably one of the more talked about ones, sure, but what about wives whose husbands leave them every four days or so to take off and work on the oil sands in Alberta for three weeks at a time? Chances are those wives have kids, need help, don't receive it and are often at times battling their own thoughts and anxiety daily. The husband might make good money working on those oil sands, but there are a lot of sacrifices involved, and one of those sacrifices is being apart from your husband or family often and having to find ways of managing that loneliness and time apart.

It also could be why the divorce rate is so high, because people sometimes simply give up and at the end of the day were truly not happy with what was going on. For me, being introduced to loneliness first came in 2008. It consisted of working on my own for the most part, going to the gym on my own a lot of the time, and living day by day on my own when my wife wasn't in the city. You see, Montreal has always been like a second home to me, but there's no place like home. I'm sure you've heard that or even felt that time and time again. With Montreal still being a bit foreign to me having not been able to speak the French language all these years, even though I was willing to try and learn it some more, it was quite challenging to surround myself in friends during my time there.

I love the city big time, don't get me wrong, but I've always struggled with French, so much so that I was urged to take a computer course in high school instead of my mandatory French credit. Sometimes we're just not made to do certain things in life and that's ok, don't ever let anyone make you feel bad about it. Chances are you can do something else or more than one thing else that another person can't. We all have different gifts we've been given in this life and speaking French wasn't one of them for me. Back to managing loneliness though.

Marilena introduced me to her wonderful family in Montreal West. They are the friendliest people on the planet. The kind of people that would do just about anything for their family, and since I was about to marry one of their family members, I was already starting to receive the royal treatment. I can't tell you how much I appreciated them inviting me over to their house often to have dinner and watch the Montreal Canadiens on Hockey Night In Canada when Marilena was out of town. If they felt extra generous, they'd sometimes order a spread of smoked meat from Lester's on Bernard Street in Outremont for all of us to enjoy. The company seriously meant the world to me and I can't thank them enough.

Their names are Mauro and Nives, their three sons, and Giorgio. The best kind of people, I mean that with my entire heart as I sit here writing this with tears in my eyes at 6:15 on a Saturday morning. Mauro and his three boys would sometimes lace up their skates, as would I, and we'd play shinny hockey on outdoor rinks in Montreal. It would bring back some fond memories of growing up as a child and playing with my dad on several outdoor rinks in Montreal when we'd go and visit his side of the family a couple of times a year.

Nothing like the cold Montreal winter air, a fresh pad of outdoor ice, a puck, and some hot chocolate afterwards. Perfection for good mental health management in the winter time if you ask me. When living in Montreal, I got to hang out with my side of the family frequently too. My uncle Simmie and Aunt Michelle would take me for lunches and dinners, and every time we were together, my uncle always found a way of showing me off to employees at restaurants. "Do you know who you're serving here tonight?" my uncle would say in his loud booming voice. "This is RJ! You might listen to him sometimes on Montreal's MIX 96. RJ Daniels! Make sure you treat him extra well tonight."

I would often return the favor by stroking his ego and saying that he should be the mayor of Montreal for how passionate he is about the city. I actually do think that though. It would be a toss-up for who would win, either him or my good pal Freeway Frank. When time began to slow down though and I was on my own more often than not, I found that the best way to manage being alone in my thoughts was to find ways of distracting myself from the loneliness.

So, I began writing out a lot of my days in an agenda. What I had to do and what I wanted to do.

I didn't think I'd be living in Montreal forever, so I figured, *Why not explore it to the fullest?* See as much as I could, kind of like a staycation outside of work hours. So that's what I did. I went to museums, the Olympic Stadium, university campus football fields, hiked Mount Royal, and more. Enjoying and exploring all kinds of different restaurants was a great part of being in that city too. Find me a city that has better restaurant food than Montreal. I dare you!

It's the best and a lot of them stay open until the wee hours of the morning too. The lifestyle is very European there. It's phenomenal. Toronto restaurants are great too, but I haven't explored them enough because my wife, mother-in-law, and mother are all great cooks, so why would I need to go anywhere else often? Plus, my mindset has changed quite a bit when it comes to food. No longer am I looking for the tastiest food out there, but rather the most nourishing in order to try and fuel me to get to the next day with a happy and healthy mindset. Like I've always said before to family and friends, life is all about management. Time management, mental health management, weight management, relationship management, the list goes on and on and in the end it's up to you on how it all gets managed best. Follow the signs and follow your mind and body's patterns for optimal performance in the moment on any given day.

One weekday afternoon in Montreal, before I was about to go into work and host a five hour radio show on my favorite English radio station in Montreal, MIX 96, the racing thoughts and anxiety were really creeping in. They were so overwhelming that I didn't know what to do in regards to going into work. Do I call in sick? Do I not? How does one mask anxiety so they could still work? I was not prescribed medication by my psychologist at the time and I didn't have an appointment with him that day to speak with him either. You see, not many people phone in sick for their radio jobs, it's just this thing that we all do. We love our jobs and you have to be *really* sick in order to not go in. Well, I was headed that way.

The embarrassment of feeling so jittery that day was suffocating me like a snake does to its prey. The anxiety was crippling, crippling my mind. To this day I've never thanked her for this, but I will now with a confession I'm about to make. Thank you to Heather for filling in for me that one evening in October of '08 in Montreal. I called in sick, which wasn't a lie if you think about it. My mind was sick, too sick to work. So, I needed the coverage big time.

People who know me best know I love the work I do and have done in radio for the last 20 years, so in order to call in sick it would have to be something major. This was. I feel like in every full time job you should be given a few mental health days off here and there. You know, to balance out how you feel. An employee might even have a better chance at being more productive that way too. You may say, "Well that's what vacations are for," and yes, that's true, but I'm talking about say two or three separated days throughout the calendar year on top of vacation. It could make a world of difference.

Think about frontline workers and everything that's gone on with Covid. Don't you think they're going to need some mental health days off? Do they get them? Maybe they do and I just don't know it. Think about everything they had to endure though in 2020, they deserve a day here and there to work on their mind, to take care of their well-being. They will be better for it. So, thanks again to Heather for filling in that day, she is good people.

This wasn't the only time that the anxiety became so overwhelming. My friend Isaac came to visit me one weekend in Montreal. I remember going to meet him at the train station when he arrived. I took the metro in the wrong direction about four or five stops when I went to go get him. The anxiety ended up overwhelming my focus, and when that happens, it leads to mistakes like not paying attention to where you're going. This is what anxiety does and that's why it's a real witch with a B as my mother-in-law would say. She doesn't like to swear so she finds alternative ways of getting her message across. Luckily, I eventually got to Isaac that day but I was late because of what happened. What's that saying again? Better late than never, but never late is better.

It was after midnight one night and I was standing on the platform at one of the metro stations after work. While waiting for the next train to come, I unzipped my bag, looked inside, and grabbed the paperwork that had been sitting in there for a couple of days from my psychologist appointments. Most of my anxiety back in '08 and '09 had to do with some self-doubt and questioning almost everything in my personal relationships. Everyone has a different way of dealing with anxiety, and if you ask me, I don't think anxiety ever truly goes away entirely. It's just something that's there and you have to find ways of managing it so it doesn't manifest into something more, and in turn end up managing you.

Whether that be managing it with medication, meditation, or both, that's entirely up to you and your doctor. There are many ways to help defeat anxiety on the daily and I'll get to that shortly, but I want to focus your attention on bringing mental health to the forefront here for a moment. It needs to be talked about more. It needs to be taken more seriously, and back then, in '08 and '09, it was still taboo to be talking about mental health for some strange reason. Not sure why? I mean we'd go to a doctor to try and fix or pain manage a broken shoulder, but why not a broken mind? Same deal.

Now though, with the help of several mental health organizations and advocates the message is getting across clear as day, that a lot of us, if not most of us will need to speak to a professional at some point throughout life, but we are sometimes too afraid to initiate the appointments or we cannot afford it. If you can't afford it, there are still free services out there for you. As my current psychologist has told me, it's perfectly normal to want to have advisors in life. Think of your psychologist as another advisor. Don't you think that world leaders have advisors? They do. They don't just go ahead and make every single decision on their own.

Social media is a great tool to help spread the word that it's ok to not be ok sometimes, but the conversation needs to keep going. It's not happening as much as it should and could be. You have the power to speak freely about it more, and sometimes it takes going through something with your own mental health to really be able to speak effectively on the topic and be an advocate for it too. My message to you is that if you're ever not sure of what you're going through, and your mind and emotions are all over the place, don't be afraid to ask someone for help.

Spare yourself the feeling of embarrassment. There's nothing to feel embarrassed or ashamed about. We're all going through something, or have gone through something before, and the only way to make the world a better place is to get your mind right so that you and the world can continue to benefit from your purpose and your greatness.

All of a sudden I could hear the metro in the tunnel approaching; my train was going to be here any second. Quickly, I gazed at my psychologist's paperwork and receipts he'd handed me again while pacing back and forth on the metro station platform. I noticed this had been either my thirteenth or fourteenth session with him. My palms were sweating. At this point I didn't have anymore coverage from work for more sessions, but maybe my wife had some extra money left on her plan for me? Nope. Nothing left from what I remember. Maybe there was a little. I wasn't entirely sure.

I was a big ball of anxiety.

I was afraid if I showed my better half, who was my fiancé at the time, that I spent an extra three or four hundred dollars on therapy for my mind that she'd be shocked that I was still even going to see a psychologist for this long period of time. It was nothing against Marilena. It's just that back then, when I didn't know any better and when the world wasn't so open to the idea of talking about mental health struggles, I thought she might get mad at me for it. I knew that wasn't like her though, but I was still scared.

The train pulled up to the platform. I decided to quickly rip up the paperwork and receipts that may or may have not been able to be re-imbursed and threw them in the trash can next to me before hopping on the metro. Do you see what I did just there though? I shamed myself and didn't want to show my wife the receipts because it took longer than I anticipated to work through my problems with a therapist. That should never have happened. I don't care if it takes you twenty, or thirty sessions, or if you have to speak to a therapist weekly for life, you should never feel ashamed about trying to take care of yourself. That goes for your mind, body, and spirit.

It's not being selfish, it's called self-care, and if we were to all do it a little more and make time for it, then, I don't want to say I can guarantee you, but I'm certain there would be far less problems in this world. We'd all communicate way more effectively and we'd all be a lot more mindful of one another too. Don't do what I did. Keep the receipts and talk it out with your significant other, no matter how uncomfortable it is. It's about time we all start getting more comfortable with being uncomfortable. Stand tall and be proud of trying to put your mind in a better place than it was yesterday.

How did I begin to see the light at the end of the tunnel? How did things improve? It took time, like anything else. I began to trust myself again. I kept trying to distract myself from the pain of the past. I would often tell people, and still to this day I express to them, that if they are to tell me a secret, I will try my best to keep it, but I'm going to let you know I have anxiety about this due to my past, and I'm on the radio, television, and multiple platforms. Sometimes we improvise, sometimes we share life stories to try and cut across and relate to the listener and or viewer. So, if I say something by accident that I shouldn't have, I can't have you scold me for it. I just can't. Just know that I will not purposely reveal something you tell me like I did with that friend in the past. It was a mistake and I've learned from it.

Currently some of the challenges I still face daily with mental health are obsession, anxiety, and depression, in that order in terms of the most struggle to the least bit of struggle. That can always change in terms of what I might be challenged by most, and I'm fairly certain everyone has felt one, two, if not all three of those at some point over the last ten months or so with the incredibly challenging year we just endured, also known as 2020. I'm sitting here on December 31st, 2020, and I think many people cannot wait to kick this year to the curb later on today as I reflect on the year that was.

I give full credit to our frontline workers who continue to show up to work and put their lives on the line each day for us. That's bravery. That's heroism, and they all deserve to be recognized at the highest regard. Those frontline workers also put their mental health on the line each day for us. When the entire world was walking on egg shells in 2020, those brave men and women still showed up to work trying their best to save lives and serve the public. I couldn't be more thankful.

Often times I wonder if there's a way we can share some of those inflated athlete salaries with healthcare and frontline workers. They deserve that money too, if not more than those athletes do, especially in a year like 2020. How do we make this happen? Who needs to hear this message? Will it get to the right person? That I don't think I'll ever know, but hopefully one day the right person that does make those kinds of decisions will end up reading this book.

It was my psychologist who was the one that diagnosed me with obsession about a year or so ago. What that means for me is repetitive behavior that doesn't necessarily benefit anything other than comforting my own mind time and time again. And unfortunately, it wastes time, not so much time that it's life altering, but enough to be annoying.

For example, when I beep the car to lock it, I sometimes beep it four times or more instead of the recommended two times, because why? Well, like anyone I wouldn't want my vehicle getting broken into and I have an obsessive fear of that happening. This also happens when locking the front door at home, and I think we're all guilty of this one at times, checking that it's locked twice instead of once. For me though, I might be a little more obsessive and sometimes check that the front door is locked three or four times.

Maybe I have a thing with doors, because it doesn't stop there. When I go to the bathroom I check more than once to see if the door is closed. I care about my privacy, so much so that it's become obsessive. I'm currently working on strategies with my psychologist and using some of the tools I've learned in previous therapy sessions on how to better manage my obsession and hopefully one day I can fully overcome it.

Life altering obsession is something someone went through in the city of Montreal a long time ago. It was a story my doctor once told me that involved a woman who literally took one hour showers every day. Fear of not being clean? Perhaps. She would go through a new soap bar I believe every two days or so. That's life altering obsession, and if she ever overcame it or managed it, I imagine it became life altering in a positive direction. It would be like getting forty-five minutes of your day back every day. Imagine that?

Anxiety will always be there for many people. The question is how do you keep it at bay? How do you manage it? By being a fantastic decision maker, that's how. For me, I was very close to travelling to Cuba in April of 2020 but that's when we as Canadians were being urged not to travel in an effort to curve the spread of Covid-19. Had I gone and taken the chance, my anxiety would have gotten the best of me considering all the potential health risks. So, staying put or hunkering down, as my uncle Allan likes to put it, was the best way to go for me, my family, and everyone else around me. It was that decision that helped keep the anxiety at bay.

What I find helps me, and perhaps could help you too, with day to day anxiety is meditation, or even, you know that list on the wall when you walk into your doctor's office, the one that reads, "100 ways to live to 100"? Try scratching a few of those off your list each day. Include physical activity into your day, read a good book, find ways of challenging your mind, do crosswords, watch your favorite movie, do more of what you love in terms of your hobbies and your work, drink that glass of wine in moderation. Again, it's all about management and moderation. Like chronic pain, a broken mind doesn't necessarily mean that when you fix it you're free of the pain for life. It just means you're good again until the next battle, but with the proper tools above, you have the ability to not only win the battle, but win the war. Now go win the war.

The depression I have been diagnosed with isn't severe according to my psychologist. I don't even fully know if I've really been able to tell if I've struggled with it. And you know what? I don't want to know what severe depression is like. I hear it's incredibly scary to go through and I wish you well if that's your big time battle. Please talk to a professional if you need to and challenge yourself to find ways of managing it. You deserve to heal.

Getting fresh air, trying to get seven hours of sleep or so per night, eating nutritious foods, exercising (which could even be a thirty minute walk per day), intermittent fasting, and trusting myself have all been steps I've taken to try and improve my mental health in the moment. And you know something? It works. When it doesn't it's probably because I've lacked something I've just mentioned. That's when you have to be mindful of why those troubling thoughts keep coming back into your mind. Maybe you didn't get a restful sleep the night before. Or you went out late and had fast food at 11:30 at night the previous evening. Mindfulness, self-care, and mental health management; those, I believe, are the key to a happier, healthier you inside and out.

12

DAD LIFE

There are certain moments in life that you'll never forget, and becoming a parent is one of them. My daughter, Madison, was born in Toronto on February 11th, 2014. When the nurse handed me her all wrapped up in blankets, I made sure to make eye contact with Madison immediately to try and establish that "Hey, I'm your dad. I'll do whatever I can to be here for you through this thing called life," connection. I stared at her for a good minute or so just appreciating the blessing of this new life in front of me. Not just any blessing, but Daddy's little girl. My mother-in-law and mother were quick to snatch her out of my hands, but I knew it was all good. The feeling of family all around for such a special occasion was incredibly delightful.

As I write this, Madison is 6 and a half. She's less than a month away from turning 7. I can't believe how fast the time has gone. Isn't that what every parent says? Well, ya. I'm no different. It mostly feels like she's 7 going on 17 though. She's already putting makeup on, slamming her bedroom door in my face, telling me that she plans on kissing a boy from her school on the lips, and, of course, there's some attitude. I can't only love half of her so I do what I can to accept the attitude part. I also try and work with her through that part. It's a work in progress. It probably will be for life though, right? I imagine so.

When I see Madison smile, it lights up my life. What makes her smile the most is indoor playgrounds, Chuckie Cheese, and Nonna and Bubbie's pasta. A smile is certainly better than a frown, but she can't get everything she wants. We all know what would happen then. Everything in moderation is usually the best practice and I have to say she's growing up to be a pretty good kid.

I don't have the secret to life when it comes to having your child listen to you. That's a mystery for everyone, and nobody is perfect at it by any means. So don't let anyone make you think they are. I will tell you what I find works for me frequently though, and that's being on their level.

What that means is don't be afraid to be a kid too at times. Communicate with them effectively, honestly, and openly. Teach them lessons but don't approach situations by trying to be a boss about it. This will help avoid confrontation. Also try to avoid raising your voice at them as much as possible. They learn with what they're surrounded by, remember that. So, if you're environment is always full of yelling and screaming and they're constantly around that, chances are they will grow up to do the same in their own family and with you over the course of the years. Yes there will be the odd day here and there where you will lose your temper and raise your voice at your children, I don't even have to tell you that, but if you can limit this, the better your child will turn out to be in the long run from a mental health standpoint.

You know, I can't wait to see my little girl all grown up living out her dreams. I don't want that to happen too soon though. That's why I'll try my best to stay in the moment with her. She says she wants to be a veterinarian. She is fantastic with animals and loves them so much. So, I can really see that happening for Madison. If it makes her happy, then I'm happy.

13

SHOULD I STAY OR SHOULD I GO? A COVID-19 CONFESSION

Let's face it, in this life the only perfection is imperfection. We all make mistakes. The key is to try and learn from those mistakes, and make less of them as we grow older and wiser. Always still love yourself in the process though. That's super important. Was this a mistake though? I often cringe trying to find out.

In late February of 2020 my first cousin Andrea, whom I was very close with over the years, passed away from a tumor at the age of 44. Most times we never forget where we happen to be when we hear of such tragedies that affect us on a personal scale. I can vividly remember this one. I was in a Hamilton, Ontario radio production studio, the size of a small bedroom closet taking in the news of my cousin. It was roughly 11:30 at night. I was at the radio station very late at the time on a day that would normally end at 7pm. This happened because I didn't want to drive home in a massive snowstorm that started earlier in the day. Up to twenty centimeters of blowing snow was expected that day and into the next morning. So, I slept at the radio station, barely sleeping of course after learning of Andrea's fate.

Andrea had lived in the Dominican Republic with her husband Lou for the last sixteen years of her life. She was born in Montreal though. The plan was for her body to be flown back to Montreal from the Dominican for a funeral service. A traditional funeral service with her entire family, which would not take place due to Covid-19.

When she was alive Andrea would normally have this smile on her face that would light up a room anytime she walked in it. I feel like the main reason I felt so close to her all these years was because of the similarities in how we would conduct ourselves as human beings. Similar to my brother and I actually. We keep being judgmental to a minimum, try to stay in our lane, and want to be your biggest fan. Simply put, we enjoy empowering others. It makes life worth living.

I have fond memories of waking up on Sunday mornings in Montreal the day after a Passover seder and seeing Andrea at the breakfast table having her Montreal bagel with cream cheese and a coffee while she held her small white poodle, Casey. She loved animals so much. I remember catching up with her about once a year in person, and she was always enthused with my goals, hopes, and dreams. I tried to reciprocate and do the same when she told me hers. We always gave each other the biggest hugs when we saw one another. We didn't get the chance to see one another often due to distance, so I imagine that's why the hugs were so big.

As the years went on my wife Marilena and I went to visit Andrea and her husband in the Dominican a couple of times. We enjoyed a catamaran together, soaked in some sunshine, and tried to just enjoy the important things in life. Family, fun, and friendship.

Should I stay or should I go? I kept asking myself. When Andrea had passed away and her body was flown back to Montreal from the Dominican in early March of 2020, plans were in place for our entire family to meet up in Montreal and have a proper funeral send off for her. We had all booked flights, but when news of the pandemic first struck and we were informed that flying was not recommended, we all cancelled the flights as fast as we could. Driving was our only hope. So, some of my family and I rented vehicles and then *boom*. It happened. Something we've never experienced in our lifetime and hope to never experience again, an emergency stay-at-home order was put in place by the provincial government, and everyone was told to stay home as much as possible for two weeks in hopes to flatten the curve in respects to Covid-19. The world was in extreme panic, and rightfully so. A lot of my family are seniors and are vulnerable to potentially catching Covid. Nobody from my extended family wanted to chance leaving their homes to attend the funeral. It was time to hunker down.

Understandable for sure. I was an absolute wreck though. For some reason I couldn't accept hunkering down. I wasn't able to stop crying for about a week straight after learning we weren't going to Andrea's funeral as an entire family. I kept browsing through pictures of Andrea and I from years past, and then tears would roll down my face onto the portraits. I began to choke up at random times of the day at just the thought of not receiving any closure. Knowing that I wasn't going to be able to say goodbye to her was what was tearing up my insides the most. It got to a point where it became too much, so much so that I just picked up and left. It was Thursday night, March 19th. I was messaging back and forth with one of my first cousins, asking her about the funeral details. The next thing you know I hopped in the car at 11 o'clock at night and off to Kingston, Ontario I went.

I didn't want to drive to Montreal without stopping because of how late it was. Normally it takes roughly six hours. I figured I'd drive the rest of the way in the morning and sleep over at the halfway point, which is Kingston. On the way to Kingston, I had my best friend Philly on Bluetooth. I was explaining to him that I couldn't believe I was actually doing this. I didn't know if it was the right thing to do or not, but my thoughts and emotions weren't going to allow me to turn around and go back home. I certainly wasn't keeping my anxiety at bay. If anything, my decision was increasing my anxiety to the max because I knew none of my extended family were going to the funeral and they were also feeling that same sense of not having any closure.

This wasn't a competition on who could properly say goodbye though. I want to be perfectly clear about that. I just felt this strong force pulling me to be there in attendance for the funeral, almost like pulling the rope when playing tug of war, but losing the tug of war contest and actually being pulled to the floor. I was losing the emotional battle with my mind. I began to bite my nails while talking to Philly—the bad anxious habit I still haven't been able to kick for thirty years now. Then I became mindful and put two hands back on the wheel while driving.

Philly could sense the anxiousness in my voice. "Can you do me a favor and find me a hotel room in Kingston Philly? Just google Kingston hotels," I said.

"Sure," he replied. He began browsing and found one that was decently priced. I didn't want to stay in a dive and I wasn't looking for anything too expensive either. I just needed a place to stay for a few hours of shut eye. Thankfully this one took last minute bookings. Philly hung up with me and made the reservation on my behalf.

I was about halfway to Kingston when it started to downpour. The kind of rain that sounded and looked like hail when it came down crashing onto the windshield. It sounded almost as if someone was throwing boxes full of clothes against the car windshield over and over. Then it just turned to rain, but my vision became affected due to how dark it was outside and how fast the rain was coming down. I could barely see five feet in front of me. The intense emotions of leaving to go to the funeral against most of my family's will started to creep through my veins. All I could hear in my head was my mom and dad a couple days prior to this very moment suggesting to me, with a lot of angst in their voices, to not go. I thought to myself, *Am I planning my own funeral here too by driving in this weather?* I decided to put my four-way flashers on and drive with caution until I could safely pull over. Once I did, the rain finally let up after twenty minutes or so. I was so relieved, but at the same time I wondered if that was my notification from up above that I should never do this again.

I was super grateful to have arrived at the hotel safely. With only knowing very little about Covid at the time, I made sure to try and spray the room with Lysol as much as possible with the can I brought with me, even though the room looked clean. The time was 3am. It was time to hit the hay.

March 20th, 2020 was the date of Andrea's funeral. Interestingly enough, our grandmother died on a March 20th back in the '90s. When I arrived at the cemetery in Beaconsfield, which is a suburb of Montreal, the first thing I was on the lookout for was Andrea's casket. I spotted it. It was all brown and looked to be made of wood. I knew it was hers because I noticed Andrea's immediate family gathered close by to it, but enough to be socially distanced. It was a closed casket and there was no time to see her since the viewing took place the day before and a couple more times previous to that. I was ok with that. I was just thankful to be in attendance.

I wanted to be there so badly for my aunt, uncle and cousins and just run up to them and give them all hugs and console them. Of course, I couldn't because of Covid. The funeral was held outdoors and masks hadn't been introduced yet, so we did what we could to stay six feet apart. There were 10 people in attendance including the Rabbi and men that were going to lay Andrea to rest. It was a quick ceremony and my immediate family thanked me for making the drive. I said it was no trouble at all. The less than twenty-four hour trip was over. It was time to go home.

I'd say the lesson here is what I recently learned from a mentor of mine, and that's mastering your thoughts and emotions. We must do that to become the very best version of ourselves. Had I actually mastered my thoughts and emotions in all this, I would have made a better choice at the time. That better choice would have been to stay home like I was advised to, listen to the experts, not attend the funeral in person ,and find a creative way to improvise saying goodbye to Andrea in a very respectful and meaningful way. As I've stated before, I was too clouded with overwhelm, which then lead to a spur of the moment decision, one that I have some guilt towards to this very day. I made my parents nervous, my brother nervous, and a lot of other family too. I'm very sorry for that. Unfortunately, I can't change the past, but I can certainly learn from it. With how technology has evolved I could have easily recorded a video for

Andrea along with a speech and sent it to the immediate family to pay my respects.

To this day we as an entire family haven't been able to mourn Andrea in person due to the pandemic. We hope to have a celebration of life for her when it is safe to do so. And whenever that day is, you better believe we'll give her the proper sendoff she so rightfully deserves. Until then, I just want her to know if she can hear me from above, that she made this world a better place, and I'm so thankful to have known her.

Made in the USA
Columbia, SC
09 April 2022